F

FACING GOD

William H. Quiery, S.J.

with a Foreword by Bernard J. Cooke, s.j.

SHEED AND WARD : NEW YORK

For the Good Samaritan

Seek and you shall find (Matt. 7:7).

One thing I ask of the Lord, that do I seek: That I may dwell in the house of the Lord all the days of my life (Ps. 22).

My house shall be called a house of prayer (Mk. 11:17).

Foreword

Vatican II is widely regarded as being a revolution in the thought and life of the Catholic Church. That it represents such a revolution in *thought* is not too hard to establish. When one compares the documentation of the Council with the statements of the Church over the past few hundred years, it seems quite clear that we have entered a period of "new" approach to the basic questions raised by the Incarnation and Christian revelation.

Whether the Council also marked a revolution in the *life* of Christians is more debatable. Unquestionably the Council has pointed toward more profoundly personal patterns of Christian life, toward a more adult performance of religious ritual, toward unprecedented involvement of Catholics in human social problems. But for these suggestions to pass from mere suggestion to implementation demands intelligent acceptance and free decision on the part of a widespread body of Catholics.

It is in this context that one sees the radical importance of prayer as a necessary condition for fulfilling the hopes of the Council. If the message of Vatican II is really to pass into living translation through the activity of Catholics today and tomorrow, that message must be made truly meaningful. To put it in more psychological terms, the content of the Council's teaching must be *interiorized,* it must pass beyond mere intellectual understanding and become part of the genuine personal insight and conviction of Catholics. Unless this happens, the informational background of Catholics will have been altered by the Council, but the deeper emotional and motivational levels of Catholic life will remain very largely untouched.

In order that such interiorizing of the Council's teachings shall occur, Catholics must learn to reflect upon the deeper meaning of what occurred in our day at Vatican II. Catholics must see that Vatican II has done more than alter some of the external aspects of their lives. They must come to personal awareness of that which stands at the very heart of the Council's teaching: the mystery of the risen Christ in the midst of the present-day Church.

If there is anything that is clear in Vatican II's teaching about Christian spirituality and Christian activity, it is that these must be Christ-centered. But if the life and consciousness of Christians are to be centered on Christ, it is not sufficient that they be directed toward some teaching about him or even toward the teaching which he, himself, has given us. Christian faith must go further and touch the reality of the person of Christ. Only then will Christ become for Catholics not just an idea, but a living ideal.

Christian prayer is *meant* to be just this: the Christian communicating personally with the living, risen Christ. Unless there be such genuinely personal prayer, it is difficult to see how the process of interiorization of which we have spoken can be achieved. Ultimately people are motivated to basic patterns of human activity by their relationship to other persons, not by devotion to some abstraction. The development of Christian prayer is an absolute condition for the realization of Vatican II.

For many people this raises a problem. They feel that this kind of deeply Christian prayer is something which lies beyond their possibilities. That religious and priests should do such they think is possible and even proper. But that the "ordinary" Christian should pray in this manner is something which strikes them as unrealistic. Such a conclusion is opposed to the stated objective of this present volume. In it, the author, drawing from many of the finest insights with regard to prayer, gives a simple approach to prayer which is both "down to earth" and contemporary, and applicable to every Christian vocation—priests, religious, and laymen alike. In uncomplicated fashion he introduces the reader to the practical means of initiating and developing an authentic prayer-life. This book should be a valuable help to today's Christians in working toward the realization of Vatican II.

BERNARD J. COOKE, S.J.
Chairman, Department of Theology
Marquette University

Contents

Introduction

"The next step for me is to begin to think about mental prayer and, I suppose, what is it called . . . contemplation?" A twenty-five-year-old lay missionary confided this to me one night as our crowded railroad coach rumbled and bucked its way through the rice lands of South Korea. The man had volunteered away three years of his life to teach mathematics at Sogang College in Seoul. He had just spent his winter vacation side by side with a group of lepers shoveling dirt and slag into railroad trucks and then running them out a half-mile-long dike, as part of a land-reclamation project. He did not consider it heroic work. College students do this in Korea during every vacation. And he had not stayed on the job long. But the experience had somehow produced in him a desire for prayer, and we talked about it for a long time.

This phenomenon is not in the least unusual today. In fact, I believe it is typical. Fully committed Christians today of every vocation, especially those most active and involved in the great struggles of our times, feel an instinctive attraction toward reflectiveness, toward spending time with God.

Should we call it "the spirit of the times" or "the work of the Holy Spirit"? Perhaps both. God's Spirit is a living Spirit and is always, in a sense, the Spirit of the times. More importantly, he is the Spirit of the future. And reflectiveness seems to be part of the future, particularly for our "emerging" lay people. Perhaps it will supply a natural balance for their new-found activity and responsibility in the Church as outlined at the Second Vatican Council.

When I was still in the seminary, we had a professor of spiritual theology who always ended his class with a provocative question. He was a small man, white-haired and almost fragile, but bursting with energy and good spirits. As class came to a close, he would toss us such mental gristle as, "What is the single most important piece of advice you can give a catechumen?" Or, "What should be one's ultimate aim in all one's activities in this life?" We almost invariably brought in answers that did not satisfy him.

One day he asked, "What do you consider, in terms of human action, sufficient instruction being presupposed, the most fundamental means to moral goodness and improvement?" My answer was prayer. His, reflection.

He was more correct, I have come to see. Reflection must come before prayer. We can pray for years and never become truly reflective. Prayer does not always force one to be reflective. But reflection—sitting down for a moment to think things over, puzzling over problems until a sensible course of action comes into view, pondering, taking time out to get a situation clear in one's mind, listening carefully to what others say and thinking about it afterwards, putting the mysterious things of life into a perspective that includes the horizons—this is the beginning of real prayerfulness, and the beginning, on the part of man, of all really Christian work and virtue.

So I have discovered something of a coincidence: that the most active Christians today are instinctively feeling the need for exactly that which alone can send them forward in the spiritual life.

Reflectiveness (and contemplation and prayer which, for Christians, should follow it naturally or, rather, accompany it) is actually being urged on the Church from a number of directions. But the urgency comes with strongest appeal from two writers whom we might call major prophets of the *aggiornamento*, though they share that distinction with others.

I mean Pierre Teilhard de Chardin and Hans Urs von Balthasar. Father de Chardin needs no introduction. A priest and a paleontologist who co-headed the Rockefeller Foundation Project that discovered the Peking Man, Teilhard spent twenty years in the Orient, and it was from Tientsin that he wrote, in 1926, his spiritual classic, *The Divine Milieu*.[1] Teilhard speaks with particular force today because he has provided us, as Father Daniélou puts it, with "the rediscovery of religion springing up in the very heart of the technological universe."[2] He has shown us how science and religion go together, are drawn together in Christ.

Father von Balthasar is a Swiss theologian who, a few years ago, as a kind of crown of all his writing and editing, gave us a spiritual masterpiece entitled *Prayer*.[3] The book

---

[1] New York: Harper Torchbook, 1965. Originally published in French as *Le Milieu Divin* in 1957.

[2] *The Scandal of Truth* (Baltimore: Helicon, 1962), p. 126.

[3] New York: Sheed and Ward, 1961. Originally published in German as *Das Betrachtende Gebet* in 1957.

was extravagantly praised upon its appearance, and called, by Louis Bouyer in *Le Figaro,* "possibly the finest book on prayer that has appeared since, say, the seventeenth century."

The seventeenth century which Father Bouyer speaks of produced *The Introduction to the Devout Life* of St. Francis de Sales, *The Christian Catechism of the Interior Life* of Jean-Jacques Olier and *Practice of Perfection and Christian Virtues* by Alphonsus Rodriguez. These books can still be read. But our age has its own spirit and demands its own books—and von Balthasar and Teilhard have provided two of them. At the center of both of them is reflectiveness and prayer.

Says Teilhard:

> If we want the divine *milieu* to grow all around us, then we must jealously guard and nourish all the forces of union, of desire, and of prayer that grace offers us. By the mere fact that our transparency will increase, the divine light, that never ceases to press in upon us, will irrupt the more powerfully.[4]

Says von Balthasar:

> [The Christian] knows that he can shoulder the burden of his Christian responsibility for the world without danger only so long as he is inwardly, and in relation to God, a child unreservedly open to the Word of the Spirit . . . , living . . . in the experience of "the goodness of the Lord."[5]

[4] *The Divine Milieu,* p. 134.
[5] *Prayer,* p. 66.

But the question for us is *how*. How be reflective? How "guard and nourish all the forces of union, of desire, and of prayer"? How be "unreservedly open to the Word of the Spirit"? We may bang our fist on the table and say that from this day forward we will guard the forces of prayer that grace offers us, that furthermore we will open ourselves to the Word of God. But that doesn't do it. Men who have tried for long years to do this guarding and nourishing and opening will assure you that the decision to do it will not bring it off.

You cannot decide to be reflective and contemplative and then immediately begin to do it. Perhaps it seems that you can, but you can't. You can't because this kind of reflection and contemplation is—at least on the part of man—an art, like the art of playing a violin or a piano. You can't learn an art overnight. There is a training necessary, a discipline— and habits to learn. In every art there are rules. But what complicates this art is that its first rule, according to both our authors, is freedom—and this troublesome aspect of the matter is an essential one in our age.

This book is an attempt at a how-to-do-it course in the art of Christian reflectiveness, prayer, and contemplation. Its aim is simply to open the door and make prayer possible, and that in a realistic way.[6] The twenty chapters are no more than twenty suggested ways to spend time with God.

The book is full of quotations and ideas from Teilhard

[6] I hope I may be excused if I use such words as prayer, recollection, meditation and contemplation in their general, not technical, sense. Thus, I hope to avoid the confusion of trying to define them. "Recollection," for instance, which most people today would associate with remembering something, and which today's spiritual vocabulary normally uses to describe a form of mind control and imagination control,

and von Balthasar (as well as from a number of other authors). The explanation for the many quotations is two-fold. First, both *The Divine Milieu* and *Prayer* are decidedly difficult to read. I have tried to pull together here the most pertinent thoughts of both authors and make them more accessible to the average man.[7] Secondly, in a matter so serious as this, a young writer feels the need to lean on the authority of others.

The author readily admits that he wrote this book partly in order to learn how to be prayerful himself. Each chapter begins with a brief "method," then fills in what might

---

is the word which St. Teresa uses to describe the act of rising above sensory perceptions and withdrawal from them in a far wider sense. The author would describe prayer "in the strict sense" as communication with God, the man praying convinced that God receives his prayer. Everything else must lead to this, and these other acts may be called prayer "in the broad sense."

[7] Six notions strike me as the main keys to Father von Balthasar's doctrine of prayer: (1) that prayer is trinitarian, and essentially connected with the Son's relation to the Father, in the Spirit; (2) that the Bible is the best source of material for meditation; (3) that the most important thing in mental prayer is freedom: i.e., for the man praying to feel free to pray as he feels moved, and to know that he may speak freely to God; (4) that divine grace is absolutely primary in every spiritual thing, and above all in prayer; (5) that it is on the historical Jesus that Christian meditation must be founded; (6) that Mary, the mother of Jesus, as archetype of the Church, is especially the mother and model of the man of prayer. Finding the keys to prayer in *The Divine Milieu* is more difficult since the book is not specifically about prayer. The fundamental message of the book might be stated in this way: that Christ's coming, the sacrament of his continuing presence, and his promise to come again make a harmony of everything in the world; all the process of evolution, all of human history, and all that can be thought of as future is only the gradual Christification of creation—including, notably, matter—with the focus of this whole process being the Holy Eucharist.

loosely be considered background material. The book is the modest harvest of a seed sown by a fragile, white-haired theology professor and watered by a tired and thoughtful lay missionary on a night train in Korea.

There are a number of striking reasons which suggest that books of this kind be written today. As far as priests and religious are concerned, discussing prayer is like discussing daily bread. It is of great importance, obviously. But prayer, I believe, has a new relevance to laymen. For one thing, there is a need—and a felt need—among laymen for a whole spirituality fitted to them, fitted to the changing religious temper of our time.[8] We read and hear a good deal about how laymen are now urged to take up their rightful position of freedom and responsibility within the Church. The voice of the Second Vatican Council is strong and eloquent on this subject. But, according to Daniel Callahan, laymen also feel "a need . . . to find a spirituality which will take account of their desire for a confident, positive, creative Catholicism."[9]

"Spirituality" has long been a specific term referring to established ascetical systems or particular approaches to the spiritual life—as in the phrase "the spirituality of St. John of the Cross" or "Franciscan spirituality." But laymen today do not want a hand-me-down spirituality designed for priests or religious and passed on to them for want of something more suitable. Nor can they be satisfied for long with what would seem to them a fenced-in spirituality, conceived in categories irrelevant to the lay state, and which would make

[8] See the Second Vatican Council's *Decree on the Apostolate of the Laity*, No. 29. The whole decree deserves to be read and studied and prayed over.

[9] *The Mind of the Catholic Layman* (New York: Scribner, 1963), p. 162.

them unable to speak the language of dialogue. They are not interested in any sort of protected or cloistered way of life. They must work out their own spirituality, a spirituality that "will take account of their desires" whatever those desires are or become, since no completely satisfactory lay spirituality exists at the present time.

And that is quite as we should expect. Today's layman is in a unique position. He is emerging, not indeed for the first time, but in completely new circumstances.[10] Today the religious atmosphere is explosive with change and contro- versy, rich and complex in its ecumenical and catholic op- portunities, thrilling in its evangelical discoveries and hopes. Nothing but a new, custom-made, and continuously creative spirituality will be adequate for a world in "a permanent state of change," in the words of Philip Scharper. Happily, it appears that the clergy is in a mood to allow laymen to form such a spirituality for themselves, to give them the freedom in this instance to be their own prophets. Thanks to the work of theologians like Yves Congar and Karl

[10] Clergymen should not complain of lay emergence. Things could get worse. In 767 a layman named Constantine ruled as pope for almost a year. See Philip Hughes, *A Popular History of the Catholic Church* (Garden City: Doubleday, Image Books, 1954), p. 85. The general reform of the Church in Europe which grew out of the Cluniac monastic reform of the eleventh century was "led by laymen: the German Emperors. The Ottonine Emperors had already made efforts, when they could, to reform the Papacy. But it was not till the reign of Henry III, a disciple of Cluny, who at the Synod of Sutri (1046) de- posed three rival Popes and subsequently brought about the election of several good German Popes (elected, for the most part, at Councils of the Empire), that reform began to operate in Rome itself." Hans Küng, *The Council, Reform and Reunion* (London and New York: Sheed and Ward, 1961), p. 92. And we might call attention to an often overlooked page in the history of lay prominence in the Church: the time between the Ascension of Jesus and the death of his mother.

Rahner, and writers like Robert Hoyt, James O'Gara and Pamela Carswell, there is ample reason to think they will be capable of succeeding in the project.

This, then, is the first reason why laymen must be reflective and contemplative: in order to work out a spirituality of their own in answer to the need of the day.

A second reason is the new freedom of speech in the Church, encouraged by Pius XII and already operating in radio, television and journalism, in national conferences and living-room inter-faith dialogues. Along with a new atmosphere of free expression goes a new weight of responsibility for serious thought thrown on those who are to speak. They must take time to think, to reflect; and all the better if this thinking take place before God's face, under the influence of the Spirit, grounded on God's written word and on all that the Christian people believe; in short, that this thinking be contemplative.

The way we state Christian ideals today puts the Christian life in a much broader and almost novel context. We once were content with such statements of our ideal as "to grow in perfection" or "to increase our fund of sanctifying grace" —correct when properly understood but rather clericalized and theological and, in the end, inadequate where lay people are concerned.

Today the *cursillo* rooms and retreat chapels resound with such expressions as "to contribute to the creative work of God and to the incarnation of the Word in the history of the world" (Ignace Lepp) ; "To increase Christ's blessed hold on the universe" and "to bring Christ to his mystical totality" (Teilhard); "to accomplish the task of unifying humanity" (Daniélou); "to consecrate the world" (Congar); "to become the vital principle of human society" (Pius XII). If a layman

is to make such aims his own—and it seems he must if he is
to be what a layman is in the Church—then he must be reflective and contemplative. How else will he know what he
is about?

It is not merely "souls" (the ultimate principle of life in
man, "the form of the body"), nor even simply "men-women-
and-children" which it is our task to save. All creation must
be saved. The earth and the cosmos are not just testing
grounds which are to be abandoned once we have timed
everyone's performance and have the score figured out. We
are meant to assimilate creation, consecrate it and carry it
with us to the Father as we move toward him.

We cannot transform ourselves in Christ except by trans-
forming the earth. This is why it matters what kind of work
Christian people do, and why work itself is holy and important. This is why childbearing is much more than "popu-
lating heaven." This world, the world we are in at this
moment and this year, is God's world from end to end. "All
things are yours . . . and you are Christ's, and Christ is God's"
(1 Cor. 3:22,23). And the mission of laity, religious and
clergy alike is, in our time, to elevate it toward becoming
God's kingdom, to make it more and more something worthy
of resurrection, worthy of the Second Coming of the Lord.
Each man is invited to take part in this mission, but he will
hardly know what part of the burden to take up or how to
do better than he is doing unless he takes time to think, to
bring the world around him into focus and find out what it
is that God would have him do.

"What I really lack is to be clear in my mind *what I am
to do*, not what I am to know, except in so far as a certain
understanding must precede every action. The thing is to
understand myself, to see what God wishes *me* to do; the

thing is to find a truth which is true *for me,* to find *the idea for which I can live and die.* . . . .What good would it do me to be able to explain the meaning of Christianity if it had no deeper significance *for me and for my life?"* Thus Sören Kierkegaard, in a classic passage from his *Journals,*[11] explains the kind of reflection we need most today. Such reflection will lead not only to intelligent action, but to intelligent prayer and contemplation.

We do not mean to throw an immense burden of intellectuality upon the average Christian. The Church is not an exclusive club for intellectuals, with the ordinary person bringing up the rear. What is required is depth. Of some people leadership and articulateness are required in addition to depth. A leader who is unreflective is almost certain to be impulsive and thoughtless, and so, for today's leaders, some intellectuality is necessary. But if a person begins with simple reflectiveness, necessary breadth and depth will follow. We are never alone, after all, or without guidance. The Spirit of God is our companion, and while he guides us through our bishops and priests, still he guides us first in our own private consciences, in our hearts.[12]

The art of reflectiveness and contemplation offered in this

11 Ed. by Alexander Dru (New York: Oxford, 1938).

12 "On his part, man perceives and acknowledges the imperatives of the divine law through the mediation of conscience. In all his activity a man is bound to follow his conscience in order that he may come to God, the end and purpose of life." Vat. II, *Declaration on Religious Liberty,* No. 3. "[Man] plunges into the depths of reality whenever he enters his own heart. God, who probes the heart, awaits him there. There he finds his proper destiny beneath the eyes of God." Vat. II, *Constitution on the Church in the Modern World,* No. 14. All quotations from the Second Vatican Council are from the National Catholic Welfare Council News Service as published in *The National Catholic Reporter.*

book is bound to differ somewhat from the conventional approach to mental prayer. The explanation of this is that we come upon the problem from a different aspect than the one found in most books of mental prayer. This book is written for any fully-committed Christian, as were the books of Teilhard and von Balthasar which inspired it. Books written exclusively for priests or religious often begin, at least implicitly, from the religious profession of the person—which then demands a certain fitting measure of inwardness and prayerfulness. For the ordinary Christian—and for many priests and religious too—it is not so much his religious profession but the day-to-day situation he confronts which demands reflection.

A man may be involved, for example, in certain almost insoluble social problems, some very close to home: race, poverty, prejudice, hunger, joblessness. He has a religious duty and a religious impulse to reflect on them and pray over them and not just go along with the stop-gap solutions that might satisfy his neighbors. Perhaps he is agonized by an alienation of his work from his inward life or from his family life. He must become reflective about it. Or, suddenly there is a lively relevance of Sacred Scripture and the liturgy to the Protestant-Catholic separation. Or, he realizes, as never before, that he is a citizen of the world, with a share in all the world's investments and liabilities, its sins and its decisions. He comes alive to the *aggiornamento* which is taking place, not only in the Roman Catholic Church but throughout the whole world. All of this calls out for thought, for penetration and for God's help. It is a call to prayer, or rather, a call toward prayer: first, to reflect; then, to pray.

A whole new world is coming into flower in a way which, according to thinkers like Karl Rahner, is totally unlike and transcends in significance all the revolutionary changes of the past. We have an opportunity now not only to change our methods, but, as never before, to expand our hearts. A few are called upon to form new expressions for the ancient faith or to devise new rites for our sacraments. But the many are invited to look out over the world, to reflect on what they see, and to grow in wisdom and in love and in commitment—and this not mainly for individual improvement but for the benefit—or survival—of the whole family of man.

We will try to approach the problem of prayer, then, from this somewhat unfamiliar aspect, namely, from the ordinary Christian's point of view. The ways to pray suggested here will not always be applicable to one whose vocation is exclusively pastoral or monastic. It is not the same thing to have a layman's task in this world and to have a priest's or religious brother's or sister's task, though in practice vocations overlap. But generally speaking, we must allow prayer to be different if it is to be relevant to different vocations.[18]

There seem to be a few pressing questions that remain here. Have not all good Christians of the past been contemplative? How does one cultivate a taste for it? Is it for all? How do you begin?

To the first, we may reply, yes, good Christians of the past have always been contemplative. In times of greater activity or of heavier responsibility, like our own times, perhaps a greater measure of inwardness should be expected. The man who, in times past, worshiped God regularly, raised his family with love and care, won his bread honorably, and gave good example to those around him certainly was suf-

---

[18] In fact, men differ from women in their characteristic approach to prayer. Karl Rahner remarks (in a chapter of great importance for pastoral theology): "We should not ask too much of men on the categorical side of religious life. A man simply does not get the impression that a long prayer is always better than a short one." *Theology for Renewal* (New York: Sheed and Ward, 1964), p. 74.

ficiently contemplative. But a layman today, who sees his
task as the transformation of this world into the kingdom
of God, who knows he must be apostolic in his own right
and not only by "participating in the work of the hierarchy,"
may feel heavier demands on himself.[14]

Whence the taste for prayer? There is no limiting its
source. But it may happen rather often these days to come
out of an experience of action, as with my lay missionary
friend who worked with the lepers. This is a "psychological
reversal," according to Teilhard:

> The Christian, who is by right the first and most
> human of men, is more subject than others to this psy-
> chological reversal whereby, in the case of all intelligent
> creatures, joy in action imperceptibly melts into desire
> for submission, and the exaltation of becoming one's
> own self into the zeal to die in another. Having been
> perhaps primarily alive to the attractions of union with
> God through action, he begins to conceive and then to
> desire a complementary aspect, an ulterior phase, in his
> communion: one in which he would not develop him-
> self so much as lose himself in God.[15]

[14] "At the Lay Congress held in Rome in 1957 Pope Pius XII broke,
very rightly, with the mystique of the canonical 'mandate' to lay
activity in the Church, through which the dogmatic sense of the
mandate given by baptism and confirmation had been entirely lost.
There has now been a return to the realization that by the fact of a
person's bearing a character he possesses a commission to the lay
apostolate in the Church." E. Schillebeeckx, *Christ the Sacrament of
the Encounter with God* (New York: Sheed and Ward, 1963), p. 168.
See also the Second Vatican Council's *Decree on the Apostolate of
the Laity*, No. 21: "[Laymen] are commissioned to the apostolate by
the Lord Himself." No. 24 returns to this theme.

[15] *The Divine Milieu*, p. 74.

For many a priest or religious—for most perhaps—it was some kind of grace of illumination, giving them a faint awareness of God's desires and the needs of the times, that led them to their Christian career. It happens when we are young, and moves most often and strongly, I believe, from contemplation to action. There has usually been very little of experience or action in their lives. But for laymen, generally speaking, the opposite may more often be the case. They "find themselves," discover themselves, in action situations, and it is here that grace stirs and begins to direct the soul. And yet, since grace is never static but rather is dynamic and progressive, all the people of God should find their vocations always opening and growing, with each day's happenings throwing light on what God wants of us tomorrow.

Is reflection and contemplation for all? Yes, for all. We may never let ourselves fall under that condemnation of Christ, "This nation honors me with their lips, but their hearts are far from me." But it is not a question of the amount of time spent or subject matter covered. It is depth, as we said, which is required. Prayer is not something that can really be measured by the clock, as Cardinal Suenens has reminded us. It does not gather up into amounts or heaps. It is prayerfulness that matters, reflectiveness, a contemplative spirit.

Finally, how is it done? To open up some methods is the purpose of this book. The Book of Sirach gives us some hints in this description of the wise man: "His care is to seek the Lord, his Maker, to petition the Most High, to open his lips in prayer, to ask pardon for his sins. Then, if it pleases the Lord Almighty, he will be filled with the spirit of understanding; he will pour forth his words of wisdom and in prayer give thanks to the Lord who will direct his knowledge and his counsel, as he meditates upon his mysteries." (Ecclus. 39:6,7)[16]

We begin by seeking, by knocking on the door, again and again if necessary. Set a time for reflectiveness. Do it every day, or as often as you feel the need. Find yourself a place where you can think, and go there to pray: a church, a hall-way, a rooftop, a park, or just to a window. Try different methods, perhaps methods of your own different from the twenty proposed in this book, and repeat the methods that work for you. Decide you will learn the art, come what may.

According to Teilhard, we must pray to become con-templative. He insists on "intense and continual prayer at the origin of our invasion by the divine *milieu,* the prayer which begs for the fundamental gift: Domine, fac ut videam. [Lord, that I may see]."[17]

St. Thomas More adds another good piece of advice. He once made this prayer: "The things, good Lord, that I pray for, give me Thy grace to labor for. Amen." If we choose to say to the Lord, "Teach us to pray"—or rather, "Teach us to pray a bit better than we do"—then let us prepare our-selves for labor. Contemplation is not magical or romantic. Like the rest of life, it is a laborious thing—immensely valuable, but laborious; immensely fruitful, but only after the plowing and seeding and cultivating, and a springtime of rain. But let us begin the plowing and seeding without too much worry about the weather. "One who pays heed to the wind will not sow, and one who watches the clouds will never reap" (Eccles. 11:4).

---

[16] Unless otherwise noted the excerpts from Scripture are quoted from *The Holy Bible,* Confraternity Edition. Copyright 1962 The Confraternity of Christian Doctrine.

[17] *The Divine Milieu,* p. 132.

1 Facing God

*Be filled with the Spirit, speaking to one another
in psalms and hymns and spiritual songs* (Eph.
5:18–19).

*METHOD: To take up the Book of Psalms, and pray, as
Jesus often did, in the words of the ancient Hebrews. If we
wish, we can mark out the psalms or parts of psalms that fit
our turn of mind and heart. Gradually the book can become
for us what it has always been for the Church: a favorite
prayerbook. Pray it facing God.*

St. Jerome, our great outspoken fifth-century teacher and
translator of the Scriptures, instructed his disciples to begin
their study of the Scriptures with the Book of Psalms.
"Why?" they asked. "So you will learn to pray," he said.
They had come to study. He taught them first to pray. It is
a lesson easily forgotten: Only prayerful reading of the
Scriptures unlocks their treasures to us.[1]

[1] "Let [clergy and faithful] remember that prayer should accompany
the reading of sacred Scripture, so that God and man may talk together; for 'we speak to Him when we pray; we hear Him when we
read the divine saying.'" Vat. II, *Constitution on Divine Revelation*,
No. 25.

Catholics today are reviving their interest in the Bible. Books and instructions on prayer are sending people to the Bible for the subjects of their prayer. A good place to begin is the Old Testament. To do so is also the advice of Father von Balthasar:

> One who has never experienced a deep sense of awe before the being of God—not merely before the "mysteries of existence" and the profundities of the world— is not yet prepared for the contemplation of Jesus Christ. He ought at least to let himself be educated to this sense of fear and terror through the Old Testament; otherwise he is in danger of coming to Christ like someone deaf and blind, seeing in Him only an example of human perfection.[2]

This is not to say that the Old Testament presents God as merely a fearsome god. As Father John McKenzie points out in *The Two-Edged Sword,* a god who does not show affection or excite affection is not a god at all. Neither can there be a true god who does not arouse fear. The striking point of difference between the Old and New Testament is, in the words of Father McKenzie, "that the Old Testament never knew the love of God which is revealed in the Incarnate Son of God. It knew the divine condescension, but it did not know that God could empty himself and take the form of a slave, becoming obedient unto death. . . ."[3] The

[2] *Prayer,* p. 128. According to Father von Balthasar, contemplation of Scripture is the first school of prayer (p. 26).

[3] John L. McKenzie, *The Two-Edged Sword* (Milwaukee: Bruce, 1956), p. 301.

psalms educate us in fear, but they also show that their writers had an awareness of God's love, even of his tenderness, for men. The tone of the psalms is rather like a voice coming from a dark valley. And it is this darkness and sense of the futility of human efforts without God that conveys to us the notion of fear and of complete dependence on God, convinced that only God can save his people. We all need such fear and such humility before we can appreciate Christ.

One may buy a book of the psalms very inexpensively these days. Carry it in your pocket perhaps, or put it on your desk. You will find that the psalms are almost an encyclopedia of Old Testament thought. Some psalms tell of the Hebrew nation's religious history and legend, some are full of prophecy and wisdom, some are blessings, some actually contain curses on the enemy. There are psalms for many different purposes, some written for personal use, some for community use, some for use at the court of the king.

We quickly discover, when we take up the psalms for our prayer, that there are some which will appeal to us especially, and some which we cannot use at all. One good system for praying the psalms is to imagine, as you pray, how Jesus must have prayed them. Take on, as much as you can, the attitude Jesus had. We can say, as St. Paul did, "I live, now not I, but Christ lives in me" (Gal. 2:20). When we pray, Christ prays in us. Even though we are praying personally and privately, we should make our voice the praying voice of the Church—in other words, of Christ.

After all, Jesus did pray the psalms. He was taught them by his mother and memorized them, sitting cross-legged with the other young Hebrew boys at the rabbinical school. And we find him quoting what he had learned all through the gospel accounts. He quotes two of them on the cross, Psalm 21:1, "My God, my God, why have you forsaken me?" and Psalm 30:6, "Into your hands I commend my spirit."

Or, if it appeals to you more, pray the psalms in the name of the Christian people of your town, or your nation, or of the world. You may even choose to pray in the name of all men. Why not? Certainly that was one of the ways that Christ prayed the psalms. Even the Rosary is, in fact, a kind of psalm-prayer form. For many people, the Rosary is about the only way they know how to pray. And it is an excellent method (see chapter 15). Historically, the Rosary was composed as a substitute for the Psalter: 150 Hail Marys for the 150 psalms. But today we have the psalms in our own language and printing is cheap. Occasionally try using the psalms themselves.

The psalms will provide us with two main prayer-tools: (1) instruction, and (2) expressions of prayer—words—which we can gradually make our own. The psalms are such an ocean of both of these that it is easier to give examples than to try to describe the treasure that lies hidden there.

Here are some examples of the first category, bits of instruction which remind us of what we believe and how we should live. "The Lord's are the earth and its fullness, the world and those who dwell in it" (Ps. 23:1). "Tremble and sin not" (Ps. 4:5). "Wait thou for the Lord with courage; be stout-hearted and wait for the Lord" (Ps. 26:14). "Taste and see how good the Lord is: happy the man who takes refuge in him" (Ps. 33:9). "By the Lord are the steps of a man made firm, and he approves his way. Though he fall, he does not lie prostrate, for the hand of the Lord sustains him." (Ps. 36:23–24) "God is our refuge and strength, a well-proved help in trouble. Therefore we fear not though the earth be

shaken and mountains plunge into the depths of the sea."
(Ps. 45:1–3) "My sacrifice, O God, is a contrite spirit; a heart
contrite and humbled, O God, you will not spurn" (Ps.
50:19). "Understand, you senseless ones among the people;
and, you fools, when will you be wise? Shall he who shaped
the ear not hear? Or he who formed the eye not see?" (Ps.
93:8) The instruction is rich and plentiful, of a basic and
fundamental kind, the kind we usually need most.

The second element is not less plentiful: words which
seem to put on our lips exactly what we have always wanted
to say. Biblical prayers teach us how to speak God's language,
to borrow an expression from von Balthasar. Thus we no
longer have to speak like children or foreigners. "I will worship at your holy temple in fear of you, O Lord . . . guide
me in your justice" (Ps. 5:8–9). "You are my God; in your
hands is my destiny" (Ps. 30:15–16). "Your ways, O Lord,
make known to me; teach me your paths" (Ps. 24:4). "Hear
my prayer, O Lord, to my cry give ear; to my weeping be
not deaf! For I am but a wayfarer before thee, a pilgrim,
like all my fathers." (Ps. 39:13) "I will sing of your strength
and revel at dawn in your kindness; you have been my
stronghold, my refuge in the day of distress" (Ps. 58:10).
"Yet with you I shall always be, you have hold of my right
hand; with your counsel you guide me, and in the end you
will receive me in glory" (Ps. 72:23).

Somehow the psalms always seem fresh and full of life.
This is due, I think, to their directness, to their frequent
use of words addressed directly to God. This quality comes
out most strikingly in the names that are given to God, to
the Lord *Yahweh,* names full of poetry and connotation,
strength and vividness: "O Shepherd of Israel . . . Our help
and our Shield . . . Our Refuge and our Strength . . . Our

high Tower . . . Our Rock of Refuge . . . Our Mountain
Fort." And more personally: "My Portion, my Share, and my
Cup . . . my Strength and my Song . . . my Shelter and my
Shield . . . my Deliverance . . . my Hiding-Place . . . my Glory
. . . my Welfare . . . you are my Father, my God, and the
Rock of my Deliverance."

But perhaps the major contemplative secret hidden in the
Book of the Psalms is this: the notion of the Face of God.
For the psalmists, praying is often described as "seeking the
face of God" and raising one's own face to him: in other
words, facing God: ". . . your presence, O Lord, I seek. Hide
not your face from me." (Ps. 26:8–9) "My eyes are ever
toward the Lord, for he will free my feet from the snare"
(Ps. 24:15). "How long, O Lord? Will you utterly forget
me? How long will you hide your face from me?" (Ps.
12:1–2) "For the Lord is just, he loves just deeds; the upright
shall see his face" (Ps. 10:7). "When you hid your face I was
terrified: to you, O Lord, I cried out" (Ps. 29:8–9). "I in
waking shall behold your face; on waking I shall be content
in your presence" (Ps. 16:15). "He has not spurned nor dis-
dained the wretched man in his misery, nor did he turn his
face away from him, but when he cried to him he heard
him" (Ps. 21:25). There are many more examples. They are
often a metaphor taken from oriental court life, where "to
see the King" meant to be his intimate friend.

Perhaps there is no better way of characterizing or describing all true prayer than as "facing God": raising to God
our plain ordinary human face which carries on it the marks
of our whole past life and the exact expression of our faith
and hope and love with which we move toward the future—
and finding, in the mysterious light provided by the Word

and his Spirit, the clear outlines of God's holy face shining this moment on me: "... the eyes of the Lord are upon those who fear him, upon those who hope for his kindness" (Ps. 32:18). "Happy the people who know the joyful shout; in the light of your countenance, O Lord, they walk" (Ps. 88:16). "May God have pity on us and bless us, may he let his face shine upon us" (Ps. 66:1). One of the prayers Father de Chardin uses at the climax of *The Divine Milieu* is "Illumine your face over us!"

Romano Guardini considers this point decisive in learning to pray:

> It is of paramount importance—we must repeat this —for contemplation to become prayer. The worshiper must reach out to the living God; must become aware of His holy presence; must seek out His holy countenance and enter into His heart. Contemplation should become a real dialogue in which man's "I" faces its true "Thou," which is God. This is what fundamentally matters.[4]

St. Thomas Aquinas described prayer—defined it, if you wish—as "raising the heart and mind to God." Taking our cue from the psalmists and from spiritual writers, we might elaborate this definition by adding that prayer ultimately comes to "raising our face to God." For the human face is naturally communicative. Most of us remember, I believe, how in childhood we often hid our face. We see children doing it all the time, especially when they have done some-

[4] *Prayer in Practice,* trans. by Prince Leopold (New York: Pantheon, 1957), p. 146. © 1957 by Pantheon Books.

thing deserving of praise or, the opposite, something blame-worthy. Peculiarly, both sorts of behavior have the same effect on the human face (when, as in childhood, it is a candid face): a rush of blood which is utterly spontaneous and involuntary.

We sometimes hear that the look on our face is our own creation, and there is some truth in it.[5] But our face is not a creation that we can make and remake instantaneously. Rather, it reflects our whole interior life. As we grow older, we control our face much more stringently. But once we are brought before the face of God, there is nothing we can hide. Our face again becomes the natural and involuntary sign of our whole interior.

Before a pagan god, a god utterly "other," a stranger god, there is nothing we can do but cringe and hide and bury our face, press it to the ground. Adoration for God, even the Christian God, has this inclination also, but it is not caused by brute fear. St. John the Evangelist expresses the final stage of man's happiness as seeing God face-to-face, without hiding or cringing. St. John means that we shall enjoy a remarkable intimacy with God at that moment. We shall realize our "fellowship with him," in St. Paul's words. We shall look up—and see God looking at us.

"Before God's face man receives his own true counte-nance," says Romano Guardini. We may understand this as something like the phenomenon we see every day—that people assume the facial expression of those they are looking at. But in this case it goes deeper, to the assuming of that facial expression which admits everything because it is no

---

[5] Paul Claudel makes a good deal of this in his moving essay on the haggard, cautious face in the painting "La Folle," by Theodore Gericault. *Lord Teach Us To Pray* (New York, 1948), p. 49.

longer possible to hide it.[6] It is at this moment of total candor and submission and childlikeness that a man receives his own true countenance. He stops "putting on." He relaxes. He becomes himself.

A man's "own true countenance" may also be thought of as his resemblance to God, what theologians call his divinization by grace. We may consider it as happening this way. The Christian, justified by the grace and life of Christ within him, has taken on a kind of resemblance to God the Son, and for this reason God the Father looks on him with love. In the eyes of God the Son, however, this justified Christian now resembles the Father—since all true sons have their father's face. Thus the Son finds the Father's beauty in the Christian. Both Father and Son then "love him and take up their abode in him" and pour out on him their mutual love. But this mutual outpouring of love, meeting in the Christian, now gives him a resemblance to God the Spirit, for the Spirit eternally proceeds from Father and Son (as we learn from theology) by reason of their mutual love.

At this point, we may think of the Christian's "resemblance to God" as completed. Now he is adopted into fellowship with the Holy Trinity. It is nothing like a legal adoption which leaves the orphan with all his differences from the family. Grace makes the Christian like God: like the Father, like the Son, and like the Spirit. He has received a new face, a true family resemblance. He can participate

[6] Father von Balthasar links this contemplative attitude with the biblical word *parrhesia*. On the part of man *parrhesia* gives us "a free, unconstrained, unabashed and quite fearless quality in our filial approach to the Father, a complete confidence and naturalness in one who has an innate right to stand before him and speak to him, to look him in the face without apprehension." *Prayer*, p. 38. Cf. also pp. 20 ff.: "Looking to God is contemplation. . . ."

in the family life or inner life of the Holy Trinity, at the moment in the darkness of faith, but eventually in the light: a son of the Father, a brother of the Son, a temple of the Spirit.

We need not be afraid to face God. Facing God is prayer. When we pray the psalms, we often face God. We turn to God and lift up our face to God, and in the consciousness of his presence and his regard, we discover and identify ourselves. There is no more wholesome Christian experience.

> *Be filled with the Spirit, speaking to one another in psalms and hymns and spiritual songs* (Eph. 5:18–19).

2 Seeing the Poor

*As long as you did it for one of these, the least of
my brethren* (the hungry, the thirsty, the stranger,
the naked, the sick, the prisoner) *you did it for
me* (Matt. 25:40).

*METHOD: To search out and try to understand what it is
that suffering people suffer, and contemplate in them the
agony of Christ. It is Christ himself who claims identifica-
tion with them. To contemplate their sufferings, then, is
much like making the Stations of the Cross.*

The Word of God is spoken out, shouted in the world
today in ways as strange and unexpected as the coming of a
thief. (What! In *my* house? In *my* pocket?) But expect the
unexpected when dealing with the Lord. At the beginning
of our era, the Word-Made-Flesh, Jesus, came in such an
unexpected way that the Hebrews, who had prided themselves for years on their vigilance for their Christ, whose
entire religion and government was built in the expectation
of his coming, failed to recognize him. We have learned a
lesson from that. Still, people may fail to recognize the Christ
today. We so fail if we do not see him in the poor and the

suffering.[1] Clare Boothe Luce, speaking to Christians about
our American Negro question, once said that if we have
never seen Christ in the Negro, then we have never seen
him at all; and we may never see him. This is a Christian
doctrine of shattering force, and it is one that we must consider as elementary in the matter of prayer: Christ is in the
hungry, the thirsty, the stranger, the naked, the sick, and
the prisoner. We must care about him there. Prayer is always
ultimately concerned with love for God. But it is impossible
to love God, whom we do not see, if we do not love our
brother whom we do see.

There is one way, of course, of avoiding this dilemma
entirely: by not seeing our suffering brothers. Superhigh-
ways sweep past the slums and rush us, in isolated peace of
mind, to our suburban homes. Prim-looking hospitals re-
move the sight of suffering from our eyes. Grim, impersonal
institutions collect misery and pain and anguish and store it
safely in out-of-the-way places. We must be willing to "Come
and see." We must be ready to search. For the poor, like
Christ, are meek and humble of heart. That is the mark of
the truly poor. Still they are more accessible to us than ever
before. If we wish, we may find out a good deal about them
without leaving our living room, through reading or listening to the radio or watching television. We will find all the

[1] "Christ's presence, however, remains hidden until the day of judgment; a proof that he does not take the place of the unfortunate as
though they were nothing but an opportunity or pretext for the practice of charity. This is not an isolated passage in St. John. It is, therefore, all the more astonishing that it has not given rise to a vigorous
school of spirituality in the Church, but the fact is that only St. John
of God has worked out a body of teaching based upon it." Maurice
Nédoncelle, *God's Encounter with Man* (New York: Sheed and Ward,
1964), p. 169.

suffering people mentioned by Jesus and in whom he hides himself.

We will find people who need food and drink, people who are lonely and who feel unwelcome, people who need warm clothes or something to wear which is at least a little dignified, people who are not well, and people who are caged up in jails (guilty, perhaps, but nonetheless miserable), or men who have been unjustly deprived of their rights though allowed to walk about as if they were free. All those listed by Jesus two thousand years ago, in his beatitudes and his story of the Last Judgment, are still with us.

We will discover, also, that the poor are often poor in unexpected and appalling ways. Their poverty often extends to their very humanity. Continuous destitution has torn ugly and irreparable holes, not only in their faces and in their cities, but in the cloth of their being and in their souls. These are the poorest of the poor. Here our search for Jesus must center and focus, for here are the people who mystically share his own last and worst destitution, his feeling of abandonment by the Father. It is the Twelfth Station.

The point in meditating on this situation is not so much to encourage money-giving or relief work, though that may result in some cases. Fully committed Christians are already doing all they can—it may seem. They are unable to donate to the poor any more money or clothes or time than they have already done. So they may say to themselves: What is the use of thinking about it any more?

The answer: we contemplate suffering and poor people because in them is continued the passion of Jesus. Like the mysterious suffering of the Incarnate Word of God, the sufferings of men are a continuing revelation or word full of mystery and wonder, a word which the Messiah has identified with himself. "Then the king will say to those on his right hand, 'Come, blessed of my Father, take possession of the kingdom . . . for when I was hungry, you gave me to eat . . . when I was naked you covered me . . . when I was in prison, you visited me . . . as long as you did it for one of these, the least of my brethren, you did it for me.' " (Matt. 25:34–40) In other words, when we see men suffering and in need, we see Christ suffering and in need, Christ on the cross. On this subject Father von Balthasar says: "Love knows that all the suffering brethren, those filled with charity, and those void of charity, are images and sacraments of the Son abandoned by God on the cross, who 'became sin for us, that we might become in him the justice of God.' "[2]

We may go to extremes, of course, in the manner of mere soft-hearted and shallow humanitarianism. But people who are unreflective often fail on the other side. This method of meditation, though aimed first at listening to God's word and responding to it, will have the side-effect of correcting this bias toward insensitivity. At least it will enable us to give to the suffering our concern and sympathy. And it will give us a chance to do what someone has described as "joining the human race," for the human race is largely a hungry, homeless and humiliated race. We must join it, at least in spirit. ("Blessed are the poor in spirit" [Matt. 5:3].) And we will avoid being condescending if we are only reflective enough. For actually we will be only returning a gift, a gift of love. "As large-hearted as we may be," said St. John Chrysostom, "we shall never be able to contribute such love toward man as we stand in need of at the hand of God."

To this contemplation of the suffering mystical Christ let us bring all the resources of our ingenuity. Perhaps we

2 *Prayer,* p. 229.

should go and visit the poor and the sick and the homeless, not as spectators but as brothers and sisters in Christ. Go there, live there, if you wish. We fear we would be unwelcome, but the secular humanists and dedicated Communists do not let this fear stop them. There may be a graceful and Christian way of doing it which we have not yet thought of. Perhaps we can find ways to share their suffering that would never have occurred to us had we stayed back home or made our contemplation in a church. As the great and fearless Abbé Pierre, the Ragpicker Priest of Paris, has said so well:

> It is not in the Eucharist that Jesus is cold: it is not in piling gold and marble and sumptuous stuffs round Jesus in the Eucharist that we shall honor Him; it is in coming to His aid in the hands and feet of children throughout the world who are dying of cold because we have no care for them.[3]

We will find, in the poor, Jesus suffering. But here is an important point to note: when we read the passion story in the Bible or hear it preached in the liturgy, we do not concentrate mainly on the gravity of the Lord's physical or psychological sufferings, levering up our emotional response with the thought of how we ourselves would hate to have to suffer what he suffered. That is one aspect of the passion, but not the real point.[4] The passion is, on the one hand, a

---

[3] *Abbé Pierre Speaks* (New York: Sheed and Ward, 1956), p. 191.

[4] "The excellence of his act is never sought in the peculiar extremity of his sufferings—no attempt is made (in the Gospels) to catalog them, to dwell on their intensity as in some later piety. It is the motive, the spirit, the attitude of Jesus in suffering which makes his work accept-

revelation of what sin and death are. But above all, it is an epiphany of the heart of God, a revelation of the mysterious desire on the part of God for our welfare and our love. The great message of the passion is God's magnificent and almost unthinkable plan for the redeeming and crowning of all creation through his own Son's victorious death and resurrection. The passion and the victory must be kept together.

The liturgy supports this view. In the prayers which the Church has canonized as her own prayers for the day of Good Friday, right in the middle of the adoration of the cross by clergy and people, we find these words: "We adore your cross, O Lord, and we praise and glorify your holy resurrection. For behold through the cross has come joy into the whole world." The Church is always able to express herself calmly, even in great grief, because like Christ, she sees the plan of God as a continuous whole. His will to redeem us succeeds. He redeems us. And even today he continues to will to redeem us, with the same love. Even on Good Friday, when we might most expect all the stress to be on sadness, the Church's inclination is mostly to adoration and wonder and trust and even thanksgiving to the just and merciful God who, from the mystery of his own death, brings all death and suffering to resurrection and meaningfulness.

And so our contemplation and study of the sufferings of mankind will inevitably issue in human sympathy, sympathy and care for real persons who can never be reduced to "objects to look at." Still we will see beyond what we see. We will hear a word full of mixed darkness and light. It will tell us what we are, and what kind of God our God is. If we

---

able to God and effective for us. And that is a spirit of obedience and of love." Quentin Quesnell, *This Good News* (Milwaukee: Bruce, 1964), p. 78.

are moved to action, it will not be that sort of frantic and impulsive action which is doomed to be short-lived.

Our starting point for Christian action and work is to be the resurrection. Then we can deal with leprosy, starvation, destitution, disease—and all that is meant by the word poverty. And we will be able to deal with it calmly, with the calmness of Christ, with something like the "cosmic optimism" of Teilhard de Chardin. For Teilhard, suffering and death must be challenged and fought desperately. But even in our final defeat we find, ultimately, renewal, since God, through impoverishment, pain, and death, provides an entrance for himself.[5]

Let us take the poor into our hearts, then, even when we retire to pray. It is the salvation not only of the poor that is at stake. God has sworn his love for them in a hundred places in Scripture. For us, he has warnings. It is rather our own salvation that is in the balance. We turn to the poor and the needy because of our own poverty and need of redemption. Those of us who are wealthy enough—in leisure and in education—to read books like this one, for example, must learn to live haunted by the Book of Job, the parable of Dives and Lazarus, and Jesus' words of warning, "Woe to you rich, for you have had your reward" (Luke 6:24). If you tend to forget Luke 6:24, write it on your wall, put it on your desk, etch it in your memory. *Don't* forget it.

When the poor and the suffering become a part of our contemplation, we have, according to St. Augustine, assurance that we pray well:

Do you want to know if God is there? When you turn

[5] *The Divine Milieu*, p. 99. For Teilhard, the cross was a symbol of the world's progress and transformation.

to Him, have you the interest of humanity in your
heart? When you try to approach God, do you bring
with you humankind and all its cares? Do you bring
with you those whom He gave you to love? If mankind
is present in your tenderness and love, God is there.

Besides, how else are we to be apostles and spread the
faith? How are we going to get men today to know that we
are God's people and are sent by his Son, that we are Christ's
disciples? By radio and television? By leaflets and skywriting
and mail gimmicks and public testimonials and newspaper
pictures? By constant preaching and pressing forward into
every new communication art as it is born? Will that do it?
It will help perhaps, but we have no guarantee. But one other
way certainly will work: if we have love for one another. "By
this will all men know that you are my disciples, if you have
love for one another" (John 13:35).

There is, then, hardly anything as important in life as
to be concerned for the needy, to be merciful and to judge
other men with gentleness and caution, never to condemn,
never to hurt a man by our influence or our hands or our
words or our silence or our absence, never to do him injury
tomorrow in order to please him today, never to insult his
intelligence or restrict his due liberty. All men are, after
all, hungry and thirsty, homeless and cold, sick and imprisoned, in desperate need of God, afflicted with weakness and
sin. If we can achieve this contemplative vision of them as
identified somehow with Christ, we will never add to their
sorrows.

At that point, we may begin to pray, and have confidence
that our prayers will be answered. As far back as the prophet
Isaias, mankind received this promise: "Deal thy bread to

the hungry and bring the needy and the harborless into thy house. . . . Then shalt thou call and the Lord shall hear, thou shalt cry, and he shall say: 'Here I am.' " (Is. 58:7,9, Douay)

Contemplate the suffering, then, not from an ivory tower or over a ghetto wall, but by taking up a position as close to them as possible, "having this mind in you which was also in Christ Jesus who, though he was by nature God, did not consider being equal to God a thing to be clung to, but emptied himself. . . ." (Phil. 2:5,7). He came to us when we were poor. We can do the same for others. We will find the poor wrapped in the mystery of sin and death, but all of this is now wrapped in the light of grace and resurrection. Find every way you can to relieve their pains and their abandonment, but above all, identify yourself with them. When you see them, say: O God, have mercy on *us*. Become, at least at heart, one of them.

God is merciful, it is true. But God is also just. And as we pass among the scrap-wood shacks where the rag pickers and their children live, as we quietly close behind us the exit door of a paupers' hospital or watch a troop of lepers pass slowly by on their way to God-knows-where (not at all an uncommon sight in this world), at these times the *justice* of God is a comforting thought. The last shall be first. Their wounds, their tortured minds, their blighted lives are not unknown to their Father. Even the hairs of their head are numbered. The day will come when all will be healed and cleansed and renewed, and every debt repaid and every hidden virtue glorified across the heavens. "And God will wipe away every tear from their eyes. And death shall be no more; neither shall there be mourning, nor crying, nor pain any more." (Apoc. 21:4, Douay)

The contemplation of the poor, as in the case of the physical relief of the poor, is neither a specially "priestly" nor a specially "laic" thing: it is a Christian thing. Priests and laymen both must do it.[6] The first work of a priest is to be a good Christian, and he may not complain simply because his day is not taken up with preaching and the liturgy. Nor may the layman complain if he sometimes has to do what may be considered more properly the work of priests and religious. For there is always a prior question: What is it that needs doing in the world at this moment? What are the needs of Christ? The answer to this will define a man's immediate Christian task and vocation.

Perhaps one practical conclusion may be indicated here. As never before, the hungry and the sick and the lonely are on our doorstep. We will pass them by and go about our business as usual only at the peril of our souls. Father Michel Quoist explains why: "All men are our brothers, for the blood of Christ made us sons of the same Father. When a member of a family suffers and dies, the other members grieve. Since we know now that millions of men die of hunger every year, we can no longer live as before." What does the author mean? He specifies: "Even if my means permit it, a mode of living beyond that which is fitting and necessary is a sin."[7] And we never will know what

[6] Teilhard, however, felt in his own priesthood a strong incentive to join in the world's poverty and suffering. In a well-known passage from *Le Prêtre* (included in the American edition of *The Divine Milieu*, p. 105) he says, "To the full extent of my power, *because I am a priest,* I wish from now on to be the first to become conscious of all that the world loves, pursues and suffers; I want to be the first to seek, to sympathize and to suffer; the first to open myself out and sacrifice myself. . . ."

[7] *Prayers* (New York: Sheed and Ward, 1963), p. 77.

is "fitting" until we see how the rest of our family lives.

Try making a meditation on it. In a moment of quiet, in a time of tranquillity however brief, bring before your eyes the world's abandoned and outcast and lost. We must do it, in fact. It will not be an unimportant moment of our day. For the moment we encounter the poor is the very moment of our judgment. That is the final meaning of Matthew's twenty-fifth chapter: the poor judge the world. "You did to Me what you did to these. . . ."

> *As long as you did it for one of these, the least of my brethren* (the hungry, the thirsty, the stranger, the naked, the sick, the prisoner), *you did it for me* (Matt. 25:40).

3   Imitating the Mass

Do this in memory of me (1 Cor. 11:24).

METHOD: To conduct your meditation in three stages in imitation of the Mass: (1) open the Scriptures and receive and accept the word of God into your mind and heart; (2) respond to the word through Christ, thankfully recalling his saving death and resurrection, and offering it with him to the Father; and (3) desire perfect communion with the Father and all men through Christ and through the Spirit of Christ. It can take an hour or be done in a minute.

I remember once seeing the well-known theologian and publisher Frank Sheed on television, speaking about the Holy Trinity. He suggested that some night when we are lying awake, unable to sleep, we think about this: What difference would it make to us if we had never been told the mysterious facts about the Trinity, if we did not know that there are three persons, not just one person, in God? Later in the program, Mr. Sheed supplied one of the "differences it would make": that if we did not know of the three persons in God, we could not understand what happens at Mass.

That started me thinking. I'm sure I had heard it before, but Mr. Sheed's remark crystallized it permanently in my mind: that at Mass the central occurrence or action is that we offer the Son to the Father. That is over-simple, but it is clear and correct. To be more complete we would say that Christ offers himself, along with us, to the Father. Or more complete still, Christ re-enacts in a sacramental way what he is eternally doing: offering himself to us, offering redemption to us, and at the same time offering himself, his life, death, and resurrection, to his Father.

This approach (seeing that the Mass is involved with the Holy Trinity) is, I think, one of the best ways of coming to see what the Mass is.[1] Perhaps (to reverse the point), it is the elusive mystery of the Holy Trinity that makes the ordinary explanations of the Mass usually so vague and cloudy and hard to grasp.[2] But, if we attend to that central action, the action of the Canon of the Mass from the Preface to the Our Father (the offering of Son to Father), we have a key and a place to begin. What precedes that action is preparation: what follows it, consequence and fulfillment. Thinking about the liturgy must begin here.

There is a kind of liturgical piety that is misguided because it is too superficial, however well-intentioned it may be. For these people liturgical renewal simply consists in turning the altar around, putting the whole Mass into the vernacular, dis-

[1] As we might expect, the *Constitution on the Sacred Liturgy* of the Second Vatican Council begins its theoretical explanation of the liturgy with the mystery of the Holy Trinity. Cf. No. 5 ff.

[2] It is also this same mystery of the Holy Trinity that is, in Father von Balthasar's book, made the ground of the need to pray, the possibility of prayer, the way to pray, the rules of prayer—all are drawn from the theology of the inner life of God.

tributing Holy Communion under both species, and setting
everybody to sing—good ideas, yes, but it is not the most important part of the liturgical movement.

The real liturgical movement has always been deeply
contemplative. It began in contemplation, and the unreflective priest or layman cannot understand it or properly take
part in it.[3] It is true that the Second Vatican Council has
now turned the altar around. The most respected liturgists
had all recommended it, particularly for times when the
worshiping community is of a neighborhood kind, and
when, through instruction, they had a common understanding of what the Holy Sacrifice is. But the Council and the
liturgists are not nearly so anxious to turn the altar around
as to effect a turning-around or renewal of heart. And the
instrument of such a renewal can be no simple technique
or gimmick. Switching things around in the sanctuary won't
do it. The instrument must be reflection and contemplation.
And any innovation in rite will then, we may hope, come
about quite naturally as a counterpart or expression of
what we gained in meditation.

We do well to remember from the start that the Mass is
not adequately described as a series of rites prescribed by
the juridical Church. The liturgy is, rather, in the words
of Father Louis Bouyer, "that system of rites and prayers
canonized by the Church *as her own prayer and worship.*"[4]
The liturgy is the Church—the sacramental Christ—praying
and worshiping. It is because the Church understands how
Christ prays that she can pray and compose rites to body

[3] Cf. *Prayer*, pp. 97 ff.

[4] *Liturgical Piety* (South Bend: University of Notre Dame Press,
1955), p. 1.

forth or make visual those prayers. What is crucial here is *how Christ prays*. Until we grasp that, at least a little, we cannot understand what is going on in the liturgy, why and when to turn the altar around, receive Holy Communion under both species, and all the rest.

It is worth noting that, when Christ prays or the Church prays, they never pray alone. Though we may "retreat" for awhile in order to pray, the whole world must be with us, in our hearts. There is, in fact, no real aloneness at all in Christianity. When Jesus instructed us to "go into our room and close the door" when we pray, he did not mean that we are to shut out our oneness with him and with his Body. He meant only that we are to shut out hypocrisy. Aloneness is almost a definition of sin, and it is certainly foreign to the spirit of the Scriptures.[5] It is misleading advice to speak of trying to imagine that only yourself and God exist, to be utterly alone before God.[6] We are not even alone at that most private moment when we confess our sins to a priest. The sacrament of penance is basically a liturgical act and

[5] "When a genuine prayer occurs within the Church, it is never an isolated event nor just an affair of the individual. All Christian prayer is Christ's own prayer given to the Church by the Spirit; it springs in us from the grace that unites us to Christ and to one another in the Mystical Body." Charles Davis, "Gabbling in the Name of the Church," *America*, September 7, 1963, p. 236.

[6] "[At times] those who pray act as if alone in the presence of God, of God in his solitude, as if they were always alone with God. . . . This is a false conception. . . . The individual contemplating in his room is not separated from the choir of the Church at prayer." *Prayer*, p. 83. Cf. also pp. 67 and 100. ". . . our salvation is not pursued or achieved except in *solidarity* with the justification of the whole 'body of the elect.' " *The Divine Milieu*, p. 143. We pray in private especially to avoid distraction, and so that we may be perfectly free to pray as the Spirit moves us.

therefore fundamentally a community act. The same is
true of the Divine Office said in private.[7]

The god who is alone is a pagan god, and a Last Judgment conceived as "standing alone before God" is a pagan
judgment. Christians recognize it as an impossible night-
mare. For Christianity, the one "to whom Judgment has
been given" is our master and brother and intercessor: Jesus
himself. Our advocate and attorney for the defense is his
Holy Spirit, who has dwelt in us all our life. The atmosphere
of the court is our Father's house, terrible and awesome indeed, but still a paternal place and not a juridical one.
Those who are lost are lost precisely for their self-chosen
isolation and aloneness, for refusing to face the fact that
their lack of service of the community was the same thing
as lack of service of God, and that their rejection of Christ
was also a rejection of his Father.

Similarly, at Mass, never try to pretend that there is no
one around you, that you are alone. We are all together,
absorbed in one common mystery and sharing in its remem-
brance and continuance. That is the reason why we gather for
worship, because our coming together makes Christ present in
a special way. "Where two or three are gathered together in
my name, there am I in the midst of you" (Matt. 18:20).
We do not come together for private devotions. Everyone
enjoys a seat in the back of the church occasionally, where
one can see all and not be seen, where one can command a
view of the whole place. It is the most private spot in the
church and thus a good place for meditation or a comfortable place for visitors unfamiliar with the service. But

[7] "Liturgical services are not private functions, but are celebrations
of the Church. . . ." Vat. II, *Constitution on the Sacred Liturgy*, No.
26. Many other parts of the document are pertinent to this chapter.

it is hardly an ideal place if you are taking part in a community act of worship.

The man who sets out to learn to pray must take his lessons from Christ. There are many ways to do this. He can observe his prayers in the New Testament or, better still, study the whole work of Jesus, his redemption. For although Christ was first God's Word to us, he also gave himself to us and has become our word to God. His whole lifework was, from this point of view, a prayer. His coming, his death, his resurrection, ascension, and glorification constitute one cosmic word or prayer. To play the role of Christ, "put on Christ," and offer his life to the Father as he did, we must pray in imitation of that prayer.

We can also learn to pray as he prayed—or as he prays —by studying the present liturgy of the Church—and this brings us back to our meditation method. For the liturgy makes Christ's prayer visible and understandable. *"Legem credendi lex statuat supplicandi"* is the consecrated state-ment of the matter in the words of St. Celestine. This state-ment may be translated, "Let the rule of (the Church's) prayer determine the rule of faith." Or, perhaps more clearly, "The way the Church prays is to be a guide to your faith." But we know that our private prayer is an *expression* of our faith. So we may conclude that the Church's own prayers are to be a guide to our private prayers, and a guide to our contemplation.[8]

We can learn to pray, then, from observing the Church at

---

[8] We may note in passing that changes or innovations in the Church's rites and prayers come from that same liturgy-guided con-templation. Thus, under the tutelage and prompting of the Spirit within her, the Church renews herself from the fruit of her own prayers.

prayer, from the Mass. In this method of meditation, it is suggested that this imitation of the Church's prayer be done *formally*. (All good prayers to God imitate the Mass informally.) To imitate the Mass formally involves spending some time imitating each of the major actions of the Mass. What are those major actions?

We have spoken of that central action—the gift of the Son to the Father. Christ himself gives the gift; and the Church (the people) gives it with him. Preceding this action, preparing for it, is the reception of God's Word through the reading of the Bible and through the people's response to the word by prayer and self-offering. Thus we may make a kind of natural unit of both the fore-Mass and the Offertory (called the "preparation of the gifts"). Then, following the central action, is the union of the people with Christ and with each other in the sacrament of love: Holy Communion. This, then, is the Mass in its three main steps. It is a style of prayer we can imitate in our own meditation.

In the first stage of our meditation, we receive the word of God by reading a passage from the Scriptures. We receive it in faith, and as members of the Church. In general, the Scripture is an account of God's encounter with man and with the men of scriptural times. But in these men, all men are comprised.[9] Therefore, I also, in Christ, encounter God in the Scriptures. My response to him should flow spontaneously. Perhaps in my private meditation I can "celebrate the word of God" somewhat as the Church celebrates the word at Mass. There, the liturgy uses incense and candles and sacred chant and acts of reverence for the book. In my private "celebration" I may demonstrate

[9] *Prayer,* pp. 133 ff.

my attitude of mind by any actions that seem appropriate.

In the second stage, we attempt to worship God the way the Church does in the Preface and Canon: we take the prayerful attitude of the ancient eucharistic prayer, first recorded in the Second Book of Esdras and used as the core prayer of the paschal celebration throughout the history of the Jewish race. The Christian eucharists or thanksgivings have taken different forms through the centuries, but the one we know in the Latin rite is a good model. Essentially it consists of addressing the Father, recalling all he has done for us in Christ and particularly Christ's self-giving death and resurrection, offering Christ then to the Father as our Savior and Leader and Intercessor and Victorious *Kyrios* or Lord, rejoicing that "through him, and with him and in him, united in the Holy Spirit, we offer to the Father all honor and glory."

Finally, we desire that this salvation reach us and touch and transform us and nourish us through the sacraments, especially through our central sacrament, the Holy Eucharist. In other words, we receive a "Holy Communion of desire" —which, in the view of theologian Edward Schillebeeckx, like a baptism of desire, sanctifies us sacramentally.[10] It completes ever more perfectly our past communions and prepares us for the next. We desire the Eucharist and we desire all its purposes and ends: union with Christ, union with our brethren, food and support for our soul this day, and a pledge of the final fulfillment of the covenant with God, eternal communion with God and men in one spirit of joy. Such meditation cannot, of course, substitute for actually going to Mass. But we may find it useful for times

[10] *Christ the Sacrament of the Encounter with God* (New York: Sheed and Ward, 1963), p. 193.

when we cannot get to Mass, or perhaps in the evening on a day when we have already been to Mass.

The method can be used also while actually attending Mass, particularly if the celebration is silent, or in a foreign language, or does not require that you be following a book or hymnal. Worship must always be a human act, one in which mind and heart are active. The more active these human elements are, the better the worship. In the end, the main value of this meditation method will be to make it possible for us to participate in any Mass, perhaps to sing the Introit and speak out in what seem to be uncongenially formalistic responses, stand up or kneel or walk in procession at Offertory, and sing at Communion and co-operate in whatever other innovations churchmen may decide on—without losing that contemplative attitude of mind which alone can make attending Mass worthwhile.

Do this in memory of me (1 Cor. 11:24).

4 Hearing the Word

A certain woman from the crowd lifted up her voice and said to him, "Blessed is the womb that bore thee, and the breasts that nursed thee." But he said, "Rather, blessed are they who hear the word of God and keep it." (Luke 11:27–28)

METHOD: To take up the Bible, ask for the light of the Holy Spirit, and then read it as it was meant to be read. Since it is God's word, try to read it in a spirit of adoration. Since it is the Church's book, read it "in the Church." Since it consists of separate books of quite different kinds, it is best to get the feel of the whole unit before concentrating on brief parts or single sentences.

One of my theology professors told the story of a priest who was street-preaching one day when a professional heckler challenged him. "God does not exist," the heckler called out. "It says so in the Bible, Psalm 13, verse 1: 'There is no God.'" The challenge immediately caught the interest of the crowd. Was the fellow lying? Or did such a sentence really occur in the Bible? Would the priest deny it? What would happen?

A man unfamiliar with the passage in question would have gone wrong either by admitting the heckler was right —in which case how could the preacher explain such a sentence?—or in claiming the heckler was wrong, only to have the man point the passage out to him and prove the priest unfamiliar with the Bible. Luckily, every priest knows that sentence well since he reads it weekly in his office, and even in Latin *"non est Deus"* has a way of jumping out at you. He had no trouble answering the challenge. It occurs in several psalms. The priest simply quoted the whole phrase from Psalm 13: "The fool has said in his heart: 'There is no God.'"

The story is a small example of the advantage of getting things, including the books of the Bible, in context. Perhaps it seems that we may overlook this aspect for the time being. After all, we have taken time out to pray. We have taken up the Bible as our book of prayer, not as a study.

Still, some study is valuable before we take up the Bible for prayer. The Bible, of course, is God's word. In it God comes to meet us. But he does not approach us as an automobile salesman might, who has a gift for "speaking our language" and a diagram to clarify every point. In the Bible God comes to us speaking a language shrouded in Asian symbolism and mystery. We can never really converse with this strange "Bible-God," we can never really confront him person-to-person, unless we live in his country awhile and learn at least a little of his language. Books to help us do this are piling up in the bookstores now, and if you inquire about "a commentary on the New Testament" or "a guide to help you read the Bible," your book salesman will give you a half-dozen or more to choose from.[1]

---

[1] Some are more complete and profound than others, but you should be able to find one that suits you. *Understanding the Bible*, by Ignatius Hunt, O.S.B. (New York: Sheed and Ward, 1962), is a series of twenty-seven fifteen-minute chapters that goes gracefully from

But do not be distracted by books about the Bible until you own a Bible and have become familiar with it. If you have the energy and time, read an epistle or a book or two completely through. Many are quite short. Mortimer Adler, who is well known as founder of the University of Chicago's Great Books program, put this as his first rule in approaching any difficult book. "Read the book through without stopping. Pay attention to what you can understand, and don't be stopped by what you can't immediately grasp. Keep on this way. . . . This is the most practical method I know to break the crust of a book, to get the feel and general sense of it. . . ."[2]

Perhaps the single most important thing to bear in mind if you are sitting down to read, say, a gospel straight through is the writer's literary purpose, his target. It is these somewhat different aims that account in large part for the differences in the books we are most familiar with, the Four Gospels. Matthew's aim, for instance, seems to be to demonstrate to the Hebrews that Jesus is the Messiah, the Savior

---

Genesis to the Apocalypse. It seems to be the most useful and readable book available. *The Two-Edged Sword,* by John L. McKenzie, S.J., is probably the outstanding popular work on the Old Testament, with *This Good News* by Quentin Quesnell, S.J., the most readable study of the New Testament. But there are many others. These books will put the Bible itself in context, and introduce you to each book. You may also find it helpful to have available some background on any particular Bible story or passage you want to read. For this purpose, the best resources are *The New Testament Reading Guide,* a series of inexpensive pamphlets published by the Liturgical Press, and *The Old Testament Reading Guide,* a similar set published by the Paulist Press.

2 Copyright, ©, 1961 by Mortimer J. Adler. From the book *Great Ideas from the Great Books* by Mortimer J. Adler. Reprinted by permission of Washington Square Press, Inc. p. 125.

promised to them in the Old Testament books. Jesus, to Matthew, is another Moses, the new Moses who has been sent to save the nation. On the other hand, Mark's main purpose may well be to identify Jesus as the Servant of God foretold by the prophets, especially the Suffering Servant described in the fifty-third chapter of Isaias and elsewhere. Luke has the Gentiles in mind, and with the help of the preaching of St. Paul (whose companion he was for a while), is bent on making the Lord attractive to non-Jews. John has a more poetic purpose, and shows Jesus as the Light continually in conflict with an unwilling Darkness.

There are many other aims in each of the gospels, but these seem to be central. Commentaries will enable you to watch the literary purpose, chapter by chapter, as it is being achieved.

Of course, this is just one good way of approaching the Bible, not the only way possible. (See Chapters 12, 15, and 19.) Some people have been well introduced to the Bible already. If they wish, they may immediately concentrate on chapters, episodes and sentences. Generally speaking, the more deeply we understand a while unit, the better we will understand the parts.

Is there not a danger of falling into error? Of course there is, if we go about it as either simpletons or enthusiasts. St. Peter brings this out when he advised the Jews to be cautious in reading the epistles of St. Paul. "In these epistles," he says, "there are certain things difficult to understand, which the unlearned and the unstable distort, just as they do the rest of the Scriptures also, to their own destruction" (2 Peter 3:16). We have to exercise ordinary caution, but the prize justifies, even makes necessary, the risk. Father von Balthasar says, "No one should let himself be turned from a direct uninhibited contact with the word (the Bible) or allow his contact with it to be dimmed and dulled, by problems and mental reservations aroused by the thought that scholars interpret a text quite differently and more accurately than he can. In any case, the content of the word is not *less* than what it can and will convey to one who hears it in a docile spirit."[3]

The Bible was also meant to be read "in the Church."[4] To read the Bible "in the Church" means to read it as a person with faith in God and in God's Church, remembering that, while the inspiration for the book came to us from God, the book was written from within the Church or, in the case of the Old Testament, from within the pre-Church. It cannot really be understood by people outside, people without faith. Furthermore, the Book belongs to the Church, and there are teachers in the Church who have, from the same God who inspired the Book, gifts for interpreting it. These official teachers, however, encourage individuals to read the Book for themselves. The Second Vati-

---

[3] *Prayer*, p. 179.

[4] "The man of the Church will always make it his concern to think not only 'with the Church' but 'in the Church,' as St. Ignatius put it—which implies a deeper faith, a closer participation and, *ipso facto*, a more spontaneous behaviour—that of a real son, of someone who is at home. Cf. Leturia, 'Sentido Verdadero en la Iglesia Militante,' *Gregorianum*, 1942, pp. 137–168—and the text of the first of the rules for orthodoxy: 'Ad certe et vere sentiendum in Ecclesia militanti, sicut tenemur, serventur regulae sequentes.' " Henri de Lubac, *The Splendor of the Church* (New York: Sheed and Ward, 1955), p. 184. "Loyalty to the Gospel involves loyalty to the Church who preaches the Gospel to us. *Sentire in Ecclesia*, thinking in the Church (which is the original Ignatian idea, rather than the less exact *sentire cum Ecclesia*, thinking with the Church), is an essential requirement for any reforming action." Hans Küng, *The Council, Reform and Reunion*, p. 79.

can Council explicitly recommends it, and popes for many years have enriched with indulgences the practice of spending "at least a quarter of an hour in reading Holy Scripture with the reverence due to the Word of God. . . ."[5]

But is such Bible reading—especially reading long passages—is this prayer? It can be, but is not always so. Much depends on how you do the reading. An acquaintance of mine, a layman, once borrowed my Bible, found an empty room near mine, and grimly settled down to "read the Bible." In two hours he was back. In good American style, he had read the last chapter first: the Apocalypse. His face was blank. His only comment: "I don't get it." My questions about what he had read got nowhere. I asked about the Four Horsemen, the battle of Michael and Satan, the pressing of the Grapes of Wrath. It was no use. "I just don't get it," he said.

My friend's experience was certainly not prayer. Could he have made it prayer? Yes, he could have, because the Apocalypse is almost a book of prayer. But first he should have had a commentary. There are excellent ones available.[6] And second, he might have read with "an attitude of adoration."

We read in a spirit of adoration when we take the Book as God's word to us. We "listen," our face spiritually pressed to the ground as it would be if we heard God's voice speaking to us audibly. People can think about God in an indiffer-

---

[5] *Raccolta*, No. 694. In the same decree, reading just a few verses of the Gospel is also indulgenced, with the suggestion that we then kiss the Book and recite "Through the Gospel's words may our sins be blotted out."

[6] One that has had wide circulation is a pamphlet, *Revelation—A Divine Message of Hope,* by Father Bruce Vawter, available from the Knights of Columbus: 4422 Lindell Blvd., St. Louis, Missouri 8.

ent way. But we cannot face God or hear his voice speaking to us without being affected—perhaps not emotionally affected but at least in the core of our being, in our will, in our heart of hearts. In this case we will pray and we must pray, perhaps not in words or not in many words. But we must commit ourselves to him if we submit to all that we read in his word, the Bible. Father von Balthasar puts it this way: "What is at stake (in reading the Bible) is that ever living contact with God who speaks to us in his word . . . , whose command exacts renewed obedience, and instructs us in such a way that we seem till now to have known nothing at all, whose power sends us forth anew to our mission in the world."[7] And in regard to the New Testament, where we are reading of the words and actions of Christ, he remarks that it "should offer the same personal contact with the Lord as men had during his life on earth; so that Scripture . . . becomes as real a medium of communication as the air transmitting the voice of the Son of man to the ears of those who heard him."[8]

Hear his voice. "Thou shalt love the Lord thy God with thy whole heart, and with thy whole soul, and with thy whole mind. This is the greatest and the first command-

---

[7] *Prayer*, p. 18.

[8] *Ibid.*, p. 68. In another place (p. 75), Father von Balthasar presents Mary of Bethany as a model hearer of the word:

When Mary sat at Christ's feet listening to his words, she was not indulging in a kind of lassitude or an agreeable reverie. Nor was she intent on acquiring ideas that suited her. . . . She was wholly alert and receptive to the word, prepared to give herself to it fully, without preferences of her own, without picking and choosing or making conditions. Her disposition was one of calmness and recollection, prepared to adapt itself to whatever was required, observing the slightest sign given by the Master and following him in his greatest designs.

ment. And the second is like it, thou shalt love thy neighbor as thyself." (Matt. 22:37–39) "Amen I say to you, whoever does not accept the kingdom of God as a little child will not enter into it" (Mark 10:15). "If you do not forgive men, neither will your Father forgive you your offenses" (Matt. 6:15). "He who hates me hates my Father also" (John 15:23). "With God all things are possible (Matt. 19:26). "In praying, do not multiply words as the Gentiles do. . . ." (Matt. 6:7).

These are sayings of Jesus taken out of context, but even at that they sound like the voice of an extraordinary person. They are meant as much for us as for the people to whom they were first addressed. In them we hear the voice of the Son of Man, who was the Voice and Word of God. They were not written down by the evangelists in order to prove some kind of theory or other. They were written, ultimately, so that the Word of God might be preserved, but preserved in a completely Hebrew way.

We approach the gospels with reverence, and with caution, because they are not the kind of history we are accustomed to. Our own factual and "objective" history books would probably have been unintelligible to the people of our Lord's day and nation. If we had been able to ask the evangelists for a word-for-word, day-by-day history of the life of Jesus, they would probably have answered, as John in fact did, "It is impossible. The world would not contain the books." Instead, they retold the story in their own artful way, selecting from the vast amount of material available just those events which struck them as particularly significant and which would contribute to their purpose in writing.

One limitation would almost certainly be the amount of sustained energy required to do any extensive writing with the primitive writing materials available in those days. The "paper" was papyrus, made from a tall, stout plant which grew along the Nile River. It was not the leaves of the papyrus plant that the gospel writers used; instead, the center of its stem was taken out, sliced up, and pressed into sheets. So, enthusiastic as the Christians were about him, putting the Good News of the Messiah down in writing would not be a question of writing down all they could remember. Rather, the problem would be to distinguish what could be cut. Finally determined on what to write, they faced the problem of turning everything toward their literary purpose. Our attitude, then, instead of tending to begrudge the writers their peculiar "inexact" style, should be that of wonder that they managed to write anything at all.

This is the way we take up the word of God in this method of meditation: understanding the context of what we read, faithful to the Church which gives us the Book, in adoration of the God who speaks to us through its pages. Place yourself where you can hear God's word, for instance, at a well-lighted desk where you can be both alert and quiet, or on a lawn chair in the backyard where you won't hear the phone or see the mailman coming, in a quiet church, or alone, "praying to the Father in secret."

At the top of one of New York's newest skyscrapers is the office of a man who practices this method of meditation daily. He rises at 6. At 6:30 he sits down and reads a chapter of the gospel, then a commentary on that chapter. Then he meditates and prays until 7, with 3 x 5 cards available where he can keep track of new insights and valuable ideas. He is not a minister but a businessman. And here is an instance where the use of a business technique—the inevitable 3 x 5 card—is entirely in order.

Success is largely a matter of thrift, said Ben Franklin.

With reservations, this is also true of spiritual success. Not that religion or contemplation is initiated by man. We know that God begins everything in religion—as in creation. We must take care never to think that religion can be derived from ourselves (a constant tendency, as Father von Balthasar points out), or approach it merely as an external thing to be judged or "succeeded at." We use our own intelligence, true, and it is part of our ascent to God. But primary, and going along at every step, is "the Christ of the heart" (von Balthasar), the "inner teacher" (St. Augustine), God's gratuitous influence on us which we call grace. But thrift is an important idea in many ascetical writings. The first chapter in Alphonsus Rodriguez' classic on *Religious Perfection* is a chapter on the proper use of time.

Thrift in the matter of ideas and resolutions is important too. To the end of his life Francis Xavier kept notes on the ideas and inspirations that came to him in his prayer time. We can do the same, at least occasionally. It is never businesslike to forget your good ideas, or to abandon upon an impulse, even disguised as an insight, a course of action that we decided upon in a time of tranquillity and vision. We must invest our time wisely, then save and re-invest the profits. And while allowing for a certain "poetry of the moment"—when we might know with perfect clarity but without being able to explain it, that now *this*, not that, is to be done—allowing such a measure of freedom, we still have to drive our good resolutions through "to production."

The businesslike prayer method of the New York executive can only be commended. He has found a meditation method that suits him, and that is more than half the battle.

Businesslike as we may be, we may not attempt a rushing

of the ripening process. We proceed slowly, not only because God's influence on us always comes before our own activity, but also because there is a natural rhythm in spiritual things which takes its course as gradually as the turn of the seasons. We can't learn prayer or grow in God suddenly, either by the best of business techniques or by retiring from life and devoting all day to prayer and penance. Even a retreat or *cursillo* can be only a preparation time, not a rushing-ahead or a sudden growth. We have to allow ourselves to be slowly sanctified by the events of life and the hidden grace of God.

When we come to speak of our side of the work, we can only say that we open ourselves—our eyes, our ears, our hearts—to his word and to his Spirit. We seek, we knock, we ask, and then we let him have his way with us. We "hear the word of God and keep it." Then we shall be blessed.

> *A certain woman from the crowd lifted up her voice and said to him, "Blessed is the womb that bore thee and the breasts that nursed thee." But he said, "Rather, blessed are they who hear the word of God and keep it." (Luke 11:27–28)*

5 Consecrating the World

*If all creation is full of expectancy, that is be-
cause it is waiting for the sons of God to be
made known* (Rom. 8:19, Knox).[1]

*METHOD: To meditate on our work. Most of our time and
energy are poured into our ordinary daily work, our
"worldly" work. Most of our life is work. But why work?
Not just to survive, not just to get ahead. Non-Christians
may do so. But Christian life—and therefore work—is something different. Bring your working day with you when
you come before God's face.*

Every alert Christian these days knows we are living in the
age of the laity. It is a time when we are rediscovering and
working out ideas about what an ordinary Christian's life
is all about. We have come to realize that the laity (who
are the Church as much as clergy and religious are) do God's
work when they work. Their work is holy, but not by the
same style of holiness which is found in the cloister or
the rectory. Lay people are not meant to be as much like

---

[1] *The Holy Bible,* trans. by Ronald Knox. Copyright © 1944, 1948
and 1950 by Sheed and Ward, Inc., New York. Quoted with the permission of His Eminence the Cardinal Archbishop of Westminster.

priests and nuns as they have time for—and then add to this eight or ten hours of work. This is not their idea. It is in and through the work of the world that lay people do God's work, as Father Congar has explained:

> As for the Church's mission, he says, it is fulfilled only . . . if creation with all its growth and increase be offered in Christ; it is not fulfilled . . . unless there be a Christian influence opening the way to faith at the level of human structures, at work throughout civilization to turn it Christward. These things can be done only by lay people.[2]

There are two important ideas here, and one of them leads to the other. The first is that by working in the world, working with matter, with people, with groups, with products and services that advance and support civilization—and by doing all this in the right way, with industry and skill—men can consecrate the world, that is, make it God's and make it develop in the direction willed by God. Work, from this aspect, fulfills creation. "All its growth and increase" glorifies God.

The second idea, toward which this first idea flows, is that all of this work, if it is properly done, "opens the way to faith," and it does not open the way by erecting electric signs which direct people to the nearest church; it opens the way "at the level of human structures." The level of human structures means the way ordinary human life is lived, in towns and suburbs, in factories and offices, the

[2] *Lay People in the Church* (Westminster: Newman, 1957), p. 423. See also the Second Vatican Council's *Decree on the Apostolate of the Laity,* especially Nos. 11–14.

way society is organized, from family units to nations and blocs of nations.

This is the fundamental apostolate of the laity, to do this sort of work. Built upon this there may be more "ecclesial" work for the Christian to do, the work of preaching the gospel in one form or another. But every Christian has this fundamental task: developing the world and opening within it a way to faith. And the reflective Christian, seeing his task clearly and simply, enjoys a modest form of optimism inaccessible to those outside.[3] Optimism, not utopianism. The world is in a bad state, but it is God's world. We may never despair; we endure, in hope.

There are men whose most important achievement at the end of a day's work is to put bread on the table. I suspect that this was the most important aspect of the carpentry Jesus did at Nazareth. But breadwinning makes both health and faith possible for a family. It "opens the way to faith."

In most kinds of work men achieve much more than just earning a salary. The job done has much wider effects, especially social effects. Giving a good example of honesty and hard work—this is vital. But what we mean to call attention to here is the effect of the work itself—the books sold, the shoes made or mended, the classes taught. This is very important. It is to this that we turn our eyes in this method of meditation: what concrete good my work does.

And, in addition, we must meditate on all the circumstances of the job: how long I work, what I am paid, other jobs I might be doing in place of my present job, my su-

---

[3] Karl Rahner explores this question in great depth in "The Order of Redemption Within the Order of Creation," the second chapter of *The Christian Commitment* (New York: Sheed and Ward, 1963), pp. 38–74.

periors or my employees, my own inward growth. This is
the particular aspect of work which the Church is coming
to see is so vital to the kingdom of God. Each man must
think about it, pray over it, if he wants to be sure that
the work of his two hands is indeed God's work, and how
much it is God's work, and how well he is doing this, God's
work.

Most men think about their work a lot, but usually with
the presupposition that their job does not concern religion
or a man's private religious life. Most of us assume that,
if we work hard and honestly, the nature of the work is
religiously irrelevant. We hear it said, "It isn't what you
do but how you do it." And so when we go off to work we
leave our religion behind in a kind of mental ghetto.

True Christianity, however, will refuse to stay behind in
the ghetto, because it feels a responsibility for the world.
Religion is *not* concerned merely with a man's private "holiness." There is no separation from the world and the world's
tasks for the Christian who prays. Father von Balthasar says,
"The contemplative Christian's view of the world and history must never be detached from the Christian responsibility for the world already implicit in the very origins of
the act of faith."[4] We are responsible for the world, and
particularly for our world, the city we live in, and very
particularly for our work-world.

You have a moment free, or an hour. Think about your
job. What good does it do? How would Christ see it? After
thinking about your work, you will go back to it more intelligently. Says Teilhard, "Never . . . consent to do anything without first of all realizing its significance and constructive value *in Christo Jesu* and pursuing it with all your

[4] *Prayer,* p. 52.

might. This is not simply a commonplace precept for salvation: it is the very path to sanctity for each man according to his state and calling."[5] Those whose calling is research, or insurance, or journalism, or razor blades, or teaching, must find time to think about the significance and constructive value of each of these jobs *in Christo Jesu.* Thus this method of meditation.

Lay out your job before you. Group around it the immediate circumstances, the people, the products or services, the methods, the prices, the clientele. See your job's effect on yourself, your family or religious community, your city, the nation, other nations. Around it all put the frame of your own life ideal and God's purpose in creating you and the purpose of the world. Find and recognize the unknowns, the mysteries. Examine the past, the present, especially the future. Try to predict what is to come, try to find your own most effectual position, where you can have an impact to the full extent of your talent, where, in terms of the world's needs, you should invest your money and your energy. Look at the dark side as well, to your weaknesses in relation to the trials you might have to face, the danger of your own malice or treachery within that framework. Then look at the eventual effects if, with the help of God, you manage to succeed in your work.

The purpose of all this is to realize the significance and constructive value of your work in Christ Jesus, to appreciate your actual Christian career, your mission in life. For the man whose life-mission is to do the world's work, his sanctification lies in knowing why he works, in doing a worthy task, and in working at it with his whole heart.

What about the practice of offering the work to God for

[5] *The Divine Milieu,* p. 67.

some particular intention; for instance, "for the conversion of Russia," "for the intentions of the Holy Father," or "for the intentions of the Sacred Heart"? The practice *can* be misunderstood—and we will explain this in a moment. But properly understood, it is excellent.

Offering your work for such intentions is part of the program for members of the international Apostleship of Prayer, and it has the backing of centuries of tradition. We can hardly praise it too highly. The fact is that, if you fully realize what you are doing in offering your work for this sort of intention, it will have an effect equivalent to the effect of the meditation we are recommending.

In many ordinary tasks of life, including those of priests and religious, and especially in many ordinary jobs, it is difficult to see exactly what effect your work is having on the building up of the kingdom of God. But if it is honest work, we take it on faith that the work will achieve "the intentions of the Sacred Heart," and so we explicitly offer the work to Christ. Doing so elevates our view, helps us work more devotedly, increases the element of charity in our life.

A good intention does not, however, change the nature of work so that driving a taxi—thought of as just a "worldly" and somewhat trivial job—is now no longer driving a taxi but has become the saving of souls in some faraway country. No, the work of taxi driving can of itself contribute in a dozen ways to the building up of God's kingdom. Looked at from the aspect of the persons alone, the persons contacted, helped, served, supported, brought together, by a taxi driver: he has a wide influence. Of course it remains true that any job can have a faraway effect simply because God's kingdom is a living Body covering the whole earth,

with members far away, including taxi drivers, mystically
strengthening or hindering other members. But if we are
the feet of the Body, let us not deny it and think of ourselves as hands and thus neglect to be good feet. St. Paul
writes:

> If the whole body were an eye, where would be the
> hearing? If the whole body were hearing, where would
> be the smelling? But as it is, God has set the members,
> each of them, in the body as he willed. Now if they
> were all one member, where would the body be? But
> as it is, there are indeed many members, yet but one
> body. And the eye cannot say to the hand, "I do not
> need thy help"; nor again the head to the feet, "I have
> no need of you." (I Cor. 12:17–21)

The value of a good intention is not that it changes the
nature of work. Each job has a dignity and intention of
its own, and there is no need to change it from what it is.
The point is to discover that dignity and that intention.
That takes reflection. To offer our work explicitly for "the
intentions of the Sacred Heart" is a way of falling in with
God's plan willingly and ever more willingly and whole-
heartedly.

There is a danger in "offering our work for some intention" only if we are unreflective about it, and the intention becomes nothing more than a label "to the Glory of
God"—rather in the nature of a mathematical sign, as
Romano Guardini puts it. Guardini goes on to remark—
which clarifies the point here—"The glory of God is not
served by doing something merely as a duty or at least to
avoid sin, and then offering it up to God; but rather by

doing right for its own sake and for what would seem to be God's own reasons."[6] In a reflective time, I can come to see God's reasons, God's own intentions built into my occupation. And I should live in the atmosphere of these reasons, conscious that I am doing God's work, working for my Father, and delighted to do it.

There is great natural dynamism and power here. It can elevate us and our whole attitude toward our work. "Far too many Christians are insufficiently conscious of the 'divine' responsibilities of their lives," says Teilhard, "and live like other men, giving only half of themselves, never experiencing the spur or the intoxication of advancing God's kingdom in every domain of mankind."[7] Our meditations on our work can be of great value. We may gradually become conscious of a nobility and dignity in selling a product that benefits men or in making managerial decisions that are both competent and Christian, and "open the way to Faith at the level of human structures." For by our work we "complete creation," as Teilhard puts it. "We may, perhaps, imagine that the creation was finished long ago. But that would be quite wrong. It continues still more magnificently, and at the highest levels of the world. . . . And we serve to complete it, even by the humblest work of our hands. That is, ultimately, the meaning and value of our acts. Owing to the interrelation between matter, soul and Christ, we bring part of the being which he desires back to God . . . we bring to Christ a little fulfillment."[8]

[6] *Prayer in Practice* (New York: Pantheon, 1957), p. 178. The question of intention is discussed in *The Divine Milieu*, pp. 53–58.

[7] *The Divine Milieu*, p. 69.

[8] *The Divine Milieu*, p. 62. While not carrying the solution quite so far, von Balthasar's view of work is in harmony with this. He presents the relationship of work and contemplation in this way: "The

The first consequence of our meditations, as many men will see immediately—granting all that Congar, Guardini and Teilhard say—is that I will see that it is my Christian duty to work hard. And not only to work hard, but to do the work well. In science, art, and philosophy, the "first rule of action," according to philosopher Etienne Gilson, is this: that piety is never a substitute for technique. His reason: because without technique piety is powerless to make use of nature for God's sake. He explains:

> Nothing and nobody obliges a Christian to occupy himself with science, art or philosophy, for there is no lack of other ways of serving God; but if he has chosen this way of serving Him, the end he puts before himself obliges him to excel; the very intention that guides him compels him to be a good scholar, a good philosopher, a good artist: it is the only way he can become a good servant.[9]

Platonic misconception consists, not so much in the exaggerated estimate of contemplation as the vision of the eternal ideas, *as in the depreciation and contempt of action,* of work on earth, which educated Greeks regarded as beneath their dignity. Christianity overthrew that view by teaching the humility of the carpenter's son who, even in his own spiritual mission, dwelt with us as 'one who serves.' Our own times have emphasised the Christian conception of work. Even more than the Fathers, we look upon action as sharing in the spirit and value of contemplation, convinced that the earthly life of the Christian, whether in ordinary family life or in politics or culture, contributes, in hidden fashion, to the building of the eternal cathedral, the heavenly Jerusalem. For all that the value of contemplation is neither diminished nor reversed, but enhanced and deepened. It means that the burning desire for heaven felt in prayer extends into our ordinary life and kindles our actions with the fire of eternal love." *Prayer,* p. 227.

[9] Cited in Congar, *op. cit.,* p. 18.

Similarly, when I work at a career of my own choosing, I must be determined from the start to do well. My Christian faith demands it.

On the other hand, when I am working at a job clearly assigned by God—for example, as the father of a family does in training his children or as a religious does in obedience to his superior, I must "pray believing" for success. We should pray that we will succeed and then believe that God will hear our prayer. Of course, we submit in advance to the mystery of this world's darkness, how God draws evil out of good and success out of failure after the model of Christ's resurrection after death. Still, for our part, we must somehow trust in our ultimate success. And this kind of faith is far from presumptuous. It is actually obligatory and fundamental and the starting point—in fact, sometimes the very moving force and dynamic—of this world's projects. By that I mean that we must believe we will succeed before God will help us succeed.

Let us explain this more fully. The concept is given to us in the twenty-first chapter of St. Matthew.

Seeing a fig tree by the wayside, he [Jesus] came up to it, and found nothing on it but leaves; and he said to it, "May no fruit ever come from thee henceforth forever!" And immediately the fig tree withered up. And upon seeing this the disciples marvelled, saying, "How did it come to wither up immediately?" But Jesus answered and said to them, "Amen, I say to you, if you have faith and do not waver, not only will you do what I have done to the fig tree, but even if you shall say to this mountain, 'Arise and hurl thyself into the sea,' it shall be done. And all things whatever you ask for in prayer, believing, you shall receive." (Vv. 19–22)

Now, this passage has always been troublesome to inter-
preters, but a book on prayer can hardly avoid commenting
on it. It may be that C. S. Lewis is correct in viewing the
passage as only relevant to saints and holy people in very
special circumstances. I would see it, however, as also pertinent to very many of our tasks, perhaps to all of them.
We know, of course, that we will be successful writers or
teachers or engineers only with God's help and only to the
extent that he wills. But for our part, I believe there is
hardly anything so important as to "pray believing" that
our poor efforts will truly contribute to the world's growth
and advancement, and truly open the way to faith in the
world.

A comparison may be made with the sacred liturgy, and
this is the approach of Father de Chardin.[10] At Mass, the
bread and wine will not be transformed by the priest's words
if they are empty of belief—if the priest has lost his faith
and intends to simulate, not to consecrate. The words of consecration are, in a sense, a prayer said believing. And they
make present again a wonder more remarkable than casting
a mountain into the sea by a word of command. In a similar
way we may come to believe in our work, and work as a man
who believes. "In our hands, in the hands of all of us, the
world and life *(our world, our life)* are placed like a Host,
ready to be charged with the divine influence, that is to say
with a real Presence of the incarnate Word. The mystery
will be accomplished. But on one condition: which is that
we shall believe that *this* has the will and the power to become for us the action—that is to say, the prolongation—of
the Body of Christ. If we believe, then everything is illumi-
nated and takes shape around us: chance is seen to be order,

[10] *The Divine Milieu,* p. 136.

success assumes an incorruptible plenitude, suffering becomes a visit and a caress of God."[11]

Take time out to reflect on your work. Bring God into your office or shop and let him look around. Then listen to his voice. It is in this listening that our reflections will become prayer.

> *If all creation is full of expectancy, that is because it is waiting for the sons of God to be made known* (Rom. 8:19, Knox).

11 *The Divine Milieu*, p. 136.

6 Opening Our Eyes

*In him all created things took their being,
heavenly and earthly, visible and invisible. . . .
They were all created through him and in him;
he takes precedency of all, and in him all
subsist.* (Col. 1:16–17, Knox)

*METHOD: To meditate on the technicolor world around
us. God shows us himself not only in the personality and
greatness of Christ, and not only in the sacred truth we find
in the Scriptures, but he also shows himself in all created
things. Jesus is the Word of God. But the visible world came
about through this same Word of God. We can read this
Word also, if we will open our eyes to it.*

St. Augustine is the great master of this method of meditation. In Book Ten of his *Confessions* this celebrated passage
occurs:

And what is this God? I asked the earth and it answered: "I am not He"; and all things that are in the
earth made the same confession. I asked the sea and the
deeps and the creeping things, and they answered: "We
are not your God; seek higher." I asked the winds that
blow, and the whole air with all that is in it answered:
"Anaximenes was wrong; I am not God." I asked the

heavens, the sun, the moon, the stars, and they answered: "Neither are we God whom you seek." And I said to all the things that throng about the gateways of the senses: "Tell me of my God, since you are not He. Tell me something of Him." And they cried out in a great voice: "He made us." My question was my gazing upon them, and their answer was their beauty.[1]

When we have some time to spend with God—and we should take time every day, and a special time every week, and a longer time, perhaps, during vacation—we may, if we have some small bit of poetry in us, imitate St. Augustine and conduct the same sort of search. "My question was my gazing upon them." Ours must be a contemplative "gazing," not just looking around to pass the time or because we are curious, but a gazing which is really the request: "Tell me of my God."

"And their answer was their beauty." In beautiful creatures, Augustine discovered God as a being full of beauty, someone fascinating and interesting, full of grandeur and power, irresistibly attractive. To Augustine, God was all this because his creatures were. We can make, and continue to make, the same discovery.

There is great spiritual force in recalling and contemplating the things and the people we love, and in them searching for God. In this meditation method, examine everything you remember that you liked or enjoyed—or would have liked—things you've seen and heard: The world of clouds thirty thousand feet above the earth, the world of holy sounds in Bach's *Magnificat,* the special world of human beauty which can be found only in children, or people

[1] Trans. by F. J. Sheed (New York: Sheed and Ward, 1943), p. 116.

you've come to know as splendid towers of all that is best and most attractive in human nature; the ordinary everyday friends who understand you and seem to value you. The goodness of God lies behind such things as these and hides, waiting for us, in the goodness and beauty of all we find good and beautiful. He is the cause of joy in all the things we find enjoyable. During your meditations, recall again these joys and look through them to God.

God loves us. It is not strange that this thought should give a man a kind of joy—if he realizes what it means. Every man enjoys being loved, even if the love comes from an affectionate old hunting dog or a puppy we have just met. We all love being applauded (why not admit it?). We all know what joy there is in doing something which people notice and are pleased with. We all know the pleasure of receiving friendly letters. These are all weak hints and symbols of the way God loves and appreciates us. Let us use them as symbols, and look beyond them to God.

Again, think of the way we love the top of a mountain, a panorama overlooking miles of green valley, a range of mountains and a glistening distant sea; the way we love a fine meal in the circle of our best and most congenial friends, perhaps after long hours of productive labor and the setting of the sun and the rise of a summer breeze, in an atmosphere of shared commitment and assured success. Could we ever love God as we love these things? Yes, if we will take time to find him in them, his beauty in their beauty, his power-to-give-joy and his desire-to-give-joy in their pleasantness, his face in all lovely faces.

From such an idea of God we can draw strength for our ordinary life, and for the life of the spirit as well, for penance, for courage, for perseverance in our journey toward the progressive discovery of truth, for our mission in the work of the kingdom, however difficult it may be or become. All of these things speak to us of God, of how attractive and worth-living-for the living God is. "Taste and see how good the Lord is" (Ps. 3:9).

The whole world of lovely and awesome things then lies open to us and may become the subject of our contemplation, from human beings down through all the orders of creation to inert matter and the atom. Into our contemplative view we may bring the cities, the ships, the planes, the bridges, all that man has built; the discoveries of physiology and medicine, physics, chemistry, astronomy and archeology; the grace of every lovely countryside, the incredible and inexhaustible fertility of the earth, the taste of food and drink, the colors of rainbow and sunset; waterfalls and canyons, mists and rain; the works of poets and storytellers and composers, painting and sculpture and architecture; feats of grace and feats of strength and speed; the sounds and colors and dramas of the animal world, the chemistry of living things; the inventions of man and his tireless search for new knowledge and new lands and planets to subdue. The list is endless. And all speak of God. We contemplate them with that faith described by Teilhard de Chardin as "the practical conviction that the universe, between the hands of the Creator, still continues to be the clay in which he shapes innumerable possibilities according to his will."[2]

---

[2] *The Divine Milieu,* p. 134. Early in the book the author describes himself as "a man who . . . has sought to teach how to see God everywhere, to see him in all that is most hidden, most solid, and most ultimate in the world" (p. 46). "It is part of the essentially Catholic vision to look upon the world as maturing—not only in each individual or in each nation, but in the whole human race—a specific power of

To make such a meditation successfully, we have to keep in mind what we know about ordinary psychology. It is not so much the thought of these things but the things themselves which affect us most powerfully and bring us most immediately into God's presence. Our aim is to become some day so practiced in this contemplation that, whenever we encounter something quite marvelous in science or something quite beautiful in nature or art, we raise our heart to God revealing himself to us in the creature. Second best is to go in search of these things, to take a walk in the park or take a bus to the edge of town, to climb a high mountain or take an elevator to the top of a building—or perhaps just sit on the porch and watch the world go by. Concerts and movies, magazines or photographs, records or tape recordings are also resources we may turn to in our search for God. The experience of trying different methods will soon let us know which are the best for us, which methods will most surely and authentically reveal to us the goodness and desirability of God.

Our reflection upon natural beauty and truth—of God's created "Word"—goes hand-in-hand with our prayerful study of the Word of Scripture. In this regard, Father von Balthasar remarks:

> The Christian must always bear in mind that the things of this world have their place in the order of salvation, and therefore are not to be considered and dealt with apart from the truths perceived in prayer. "Every creature of God is good" . . . it is "sanctified by

knowing and loving whose transfigured term is charity, but whose roots and elemental sap lie in the discovery and the love of everything that is true and beautiful in creation" (p. 97).

the word of God and prayer" (1 Tim. 4:4–5). For this reason, contemplation of the Word which sanctifies is necessary, if we are to use God's creatures for God's purpose.[3]

Thus, only when we see things as related inseparably to Christ and to his salvation do we see things truly, as they are. St. Paul wrote about this idea, in several places in his letters—but it is my impression that it is seldom preached about in our churches today. Paul writes to the Ephesians, "It was God's loving design, centered in Christ, to give history its fulfillment by resuming everything in him, all that is in Heaven, all that is on earth, summed up in him" (Eph. 1:9–10, Knox). And to the Colossians, "Yes, in him all created things took their being, heavenly and earthly, visible and invisible. . . . They were all created through him and in him; he takes precedency of all, and in him all subsist." (Col. 1:16–17, Knox)

With St. Paul's words we move from what very well might have been a pre-Christian contemplation to a contemplation thoroughly Christian. For us everything in the world and in history points to Christ—if we understand these words of St. Paul; and if we recall what we know about the Holy Trinity.

We may think of it this way: the power by which we move toward God is the power of the Holy Spirit within us. The Way that lies open to God, the only way, is Jesus, God's Son. The destination: our Father's house. Power, Way, Destination: Spirit, Son, Father.

When we take up a way to God, Jesus is always that way, whether it be the book of the Scriptures that guides us or the book of the visible creation. Religious truth, therefore,

[3] *Prayer,* p. 65.

transforms and sanctifies the truth of creation. All that is in
heaven and on earth and all history is summed up in, and
points to, Christ. This is what is meant by "in him all created
things took their being . . . and subsist."

Creation then, the world of natural things around us, can
be much more deeply understood if we know the doctrine
of the Holy Trinity. When the Father speaks a word of
creation—for instance, "Let there be light"—it is, in a sense,
his Son which he speaks. "In the beginning was the Word
. . . all things were made through him" (John 1:1–3). If the
Father speaks the Word more strongly, he calls into existence
a higher form of being, plant life. He speaks more strongly
still in animal life, and still more emphatically in rational
life. These are not just orders or degrees of existence, they
reflect degrees of participation in God's Word. Finally, when
the Father speaks to our world fully, when he sends his Word
to us with all his strength, the Word becomes flesh and
blood, and standing before us is a man who tops out and
crowns creation. His mother calls him Jesus. The alert Jews
recognize him as their Christ. But to the Heavenly Father,
he is "my Son; this day have I begotten you" (Ps. 2:7).

Knowing this, we enjoy a kind of privileged knowledge,
that everywhere we look, in every direction, there is the
Word of God. "They were all created through him and in
him; he takes precedency of all, and in him all subsist."
Every touch of beauty or goodness in creatures, every grace,
every joy, speaks the Word of God. There is no room then
for a fear of creatures, that they are traps to catch and ruin
us. We may choose to fear ourselves and our proved weakness. But for creatures we may—and must—have reverence.
They come from God and they speak of God.

St. Augustine, the master of this meditation method, returns to this theme in his book on the Holy Trinity. His remarks are worth quoting in full. Earlier he showed us how to begin our search. Here he describes how we might expand it and exploit it:

> Look again, and see, if you can. You certainly do not love anything except what is good, since good is the earth, with the loftiness of its plains; and good is an estate that is pleasant and fertile; and good is a house that is arranged in due proportions and is spacious and bright; and good are animal and animate bodies; and good is air that is temperate and healthful; and good is food that is agreeable and fit for health; and good is health, without pains or lassitude; and good is the countenance of man that is disposed in fit proportions, and is cheerful in look, and bright in color; and good is the mind of a friend, with the sweetness of agreement, and with the confidence of love; and good is a righteous man; and good are riches since they are readily useful; and good is the heaven, with its sun, and moon, and stars; and good are the angels, by their holy obedience; and good is discourse that sweetly teaches and suitably admonishes the hearer; and good is a poem that is harmonious in its numbers and weighty in its sense. And why add yet more and more? This thing is good and that good, but take away this and that, and regard good itself if you can; so will you see God, not good by a good that is other than Himself, but the good of all good. So God is to be loved, not as this and that good, but as the good itself. . . . Not a good mind, or a good angel, or a good heaven, but the good Good.

This is the way, according to Augustine, to come "to appreciate God"—if I may use the term; it really means "to love God," a very hard concept for many men if we are honest about how we use words. Love? Love God? Yes. We may not find words for our love of the kind the psalmists used: "O God, I love thee, I love thee." Words like this may not fit our personal vocabulary at all. Perhaps we are more like St. Paul. Paul could not often bring himself to write explicitly of his love, however he may have prayed in private. I find over fifty striking instances in the epistles where St. Paul speaks of how good Christ has been to him, how Christ has loved him, but only once can I find him unambiguously speaking of his own "love for Christ."[4]

Still Paul writes eloquently and passionately of how Christ has loved him, and from Paul pours forth the response of action and promises of action. It bursts from him again and again, this desire to do something in return for Christ's love: to share his sufferings, to work for the Lord, to serve the Lord, to be a fool for Christ's sake, a slave for Christ, hanging on the cross with Christ.

This may be the way we choose to pray—by action and by promises of action and by decision and commitment— the way many a good father of a family shows his love for his family. Others will use both words and actions. But words alone or just feelings alone are sterile. "If anyone love me, he will keep my word" (John 14:23). "My mother and my

---

[4] This one clear instance is in Phil. 3:8: "There is nothing I do not write down as loss compared with the high privilege of knowing Christ Jesus, my Lord; *for love of him I have lost everything*, treat everything else as refuse, if I may have Christ to my credit" (Knox). Several other instances may be alleged, depending on what translation you use—but strikingly few.

brethren are they who hear the word of God and act upon it" (Luke 8:21).

> *In him all created things took their being,*
> *heavenly and earthly, visible and invisible. . . .*
> *They were all created through him and in him;*
> *he takes precedency of all, and in him all*
> *subsist.* (Col. 1:16–17, Knox)

7 Outflanking Inertia

Rejoice always. Pray without ceasing. In all things give thanks; for this is the will of God in Christ Jesus regarding you all. Do not extinguish the Spirit. (1 Thess. 5:16–19)

METHOD: To make use of mnemonic or numerical devices or memorized formulas which will help you make your prayer continuous and less distracted. Public speakers and actors, because they have a lot to remember, often construct hint-systems which are easy to recall. Contemplation is far different from public speaking or acting. But mental dullness and forgetfulness and distraction are a problem common to both types of activity. The solutions are similar also.

Religion can be over-spiritualized. We are not angels. When a man prays, the whole of him prays: his mind and his heart, his hands and his knees, his head, his feet, and his memory and his imagination. If you want to teach yourself contemplation, bring all these parts of you along to the training room. Teilhard de Chardin says in another connection, "We are constantly forgetting that the supernatural is a ferment, a soul, and not a complete and finished organism. Its role is to transform 'nature'; but it cannot do so apart from the matter which nature provides it with."[1]

[1] *The Divine Milieu,* p. 152.

As soon as we begin the training—in fact, the very moment we begin—we will quickly see which "parts" or elements of ourselves are going to need the most discipline. The ordinary man who decides he is going to pray has already set his mind and heart initially on God. Hands and knees, head and feet: they are no trouble. They will submit obediently to training. But memory? Imagination? Here is the problem. We often find we cannot, we simply *cannot,* concentrate.

And yet, this wild memory of mine, this elusive and irresponsible imagination, these are "the matter which nature provides (me) with." It is the work of grace to transform this also, this disobedient memory, this incorrigible imagination. The question: how?

A woman once told me how amazed she was at her husband's ability to pray. As soon as the Sunday Mass was over, she said she usually found herself ready to leave the church, with all her prayers said and all her prayer ideas exhausted. But at her side her husband knelt absorbed in his prayers, without even the help of a book. Sometimes she would leave the pew and wait for him in the vestibule. After five or ten minutes, he would come strolling out as if nothing extraordinary had happened.

Finally one day the woman could stand it no longer, and she asked him, "What on earth are you praying about so long after Mass? How do you do it? It's the worst time in the world for me to pray." Her husband answered that he was just using a little system he had learned from the brothers who taught him in high school. He said that when he wanted to pray, he would just take the word *baptism,* and to each of the letters of the word was attached a prayer idea. When he had used up the idea attached to the letter *b* (whatever it was), he would go on to *a,* then *p* and so on. Apparently he never tired of the same old set of prayer-ideas. He claimed that he often would not get through them all by the time he had to leave.

Who has not knelt to pray and found his mind a blank and his imagination a thousand miles away? Or who has not found himself trapped some place listening to the drone of an unintelligible and seemingly endless lecture or sermon, and wishing he could find some way to occupy his mind? It is a common experience. We can spend the time with God, if we wish, and many people can learn to outflank their distractions, at least to some extent, and without mental strain.

We might as well begin with the key-word or hint-word used by the man in the story: baptism. In a few minutes, anyone can convert it into a set of seven prayer subjects—and a set made out by yourself is probably better than any supplied to you. But for a few examples:

B	Business Associates	Brazil	Benevolence
A	Acquaintances	Australia	Appreciativeness
P	Parents	Poland	Patience
T	The Troubled	Thailand	Thanksgiving
I	The Injured	India	Impetration
S	The Suffering	Sweden	Sympathy
M	The Mentally Ill	Mexico	Moderation

All this may appear at first to be a little childish. It provides a framework, nothing more, for those who may need one. Within the frame, you are on your own. One system would be simply to recite a number of Hail Marys for each category, begging God through Mary to bless the people you may be praying for, or give you the virtue recalled. When-

ever we recite Hail Marys or any other prayer, we can attend
to each word of the prayer and mean every word we say; or,
we may use the sacred words of the prayer as a kind of psalm
or song, a melody of words which we employ to carry our
general prayerful attitude. But remember that any prayer
formula is not prayer "by itself," that is, merely by being
recited. Unless our heart is in the prayer in some way, we
are only making sounds or going through meaningless mo-
tions. This is not prayer at all. It is not only inhuman and
superstitious, it can be offensive to God, an abuse of his
word.

A better use for the *baptism* hints would be to take your
time with each item, and speak to God freely and simply
about it. Best of all is to work out a system all your own.
Thus you will be able to pray quite well any time you have
an opportunity, and for a longer or shorter time. Tailor
your solution to your problem. If you have an imagination
of the vivid and over-active sort, where a kind of psychological inertia keeps churning up one distraction after another, set your strong imagination to the job of harnessing
its own powers. Figure out a method by which you can
pray. Grace is needed when we pray, but grace seldom
annuls the laws of psychology.

Memory devices in the form of a series of numbers are
also useful. For example, when we are at a loss how to conduct ourselves for a given period of prayer, we may decide
on the number "3." Offer to God three requests, three
thanksgivings, three words of praise. If we are making a short
visit to a church, such a method may be useful. It helps us
to connect quickly the ordinary ups-and-downs of life with
what is permanent: God and his divine plan.

Three requests: when we stop to think what they might

be, our hopes and disappointments fall into ranks—*this* matters, *that* is a trifle. Three thanksgivings: we almost always find it difficult to decide, not whether there is anything good happening to us, but what to be most thankful for. Here again order rises out of the chaos of our subconscious. Three words of praise: for the beauty of the mountainside, for the power of the storm, for the sweetness of the breeze that follows the rain. It takes us out of ourselves, which is a good place to be once in a while.

I read somewhere recently of the way a child described the prayer he made after his first Holy Communion. First he had asked God to bless his family and his friends. Then he recited his A-B-C's. And he capped it all by telling God a ghost story.

Obviously, of such is the kingdom of heaven. It is childish, and the details of our lives are not A-B-C's. All the more reason why we should pray over these details. They make up the road we are walking at the moment, and that road leads to God and to the coming of his kingdom. As with any road, it is the destination, not the route, that determines its importance. We hesitate to take a simple route, perhaps? Giants of theology do not. The eminent theologian Karl Rahner says:

> It is only by grace that we can learn how to pray, but our willingness to pray and our perseverance in praying play an important part. We must learn to concentrate, in interior silence, on what we are about to do, namely, to lift up our hearts. We must learn to speak to God without using set words; we must speak to Him of our necessities, of our daily life, in particular of that secret resistance against speaking to Him about our duties.

We must speak to Him of our loved ones, of our moods, of the world and its needs, of the dead who have gone before us, and of Himself. Our words must tell of His greatness and distance, incomprehensible and yet wonderful, of His truth in contrast to our untruth, of His love and our selfishness.[2]

Our willingness to pray and our perseverance, these are very important indeed. If we know that we can expect our attention span to be pretty small—and it shrinks when we are tired or upset or in love or enthusiastic about something —then it is good to use such human supports as these prayer-hint devices to keep us at it.

Hidden among the back pages of the classic handbook for retreat masters written four hundred years ago by St. Ignatius Loyola[3] are three spiritual exercises which come to exactly what we are speaking about here. They take into account the typical distractedness of the human mind and make use of compensating devices which are readily available. In the first of these "Methods of Prayer," Ignatius suggests that we use the ten commandments, the seven deadly sins, the three powers of the soul (memory, intellect, and will), and the five senses of the body. These are the handles by which we hang on to our prayer, something all the people of that time knew by memory. By simply recalling the numbers 10, 7, 3, 5 they could meditate profitably for a long

[2] Karl Rahner, *Happiness through Prayer* (Westminster: Newman, 1958), p. 51.

[3] This book is known as *The Spiritual Exercises*. It was first approved for publication in 1548, and it climaxed a growing popular concern for methodical mental prayer that extended over some four centuries. Editions of the text or commentaries have averaged one a month over the four hundred years since its appearance.

time, and when distracted, quickly locate themselves and resume their meditation. Ignatius says we are to spend the time it would take to say three Our Fathers and three Hail Marys on each of the twenty-five subjects—delaying longer, of course, if we choose. After thinking about each subject, we raise our heart to God and then go on.

His second method—perhaps the most famous—makes use of any or all the prayers we know by heart. The system is to consider these prayers word by word and phrase by phrase. If one is moved to prayer by one or two of the words, "he should not be axious to pass on, even though the hour be spent on that one word." It is this remark of St. Ignatius, I think, which has made the system, well known as "The Second Method of Prayer," so famous. It allows for perfect flexibility under the guidance of the Holy Spirit and for the inclinations of temperament which inevitably play a big part in meditation.

The third system in the book, perhaps the most curious, is by way of rhythm. It is to say some vocal prayer so slowly and thoughtfully that each time we breathe we say only one word. It can keep us busy with the praise of God, in a quiet and relaxed way, when everything else fails. It is not "just a gimmick." It answers a serious spiritual need. Associating breathing with meditation is also one of the fundamentals of the ancient Indian discipline known as Yoga, and was in use among the primitive Christian monks of the desert.[4]

Experiment with different methods of prayer until you find one that suits you, at least for the time being. But above all, maintain your freedom. There are times when every sensible man knows he should not pray and he cannot pray: when there is work which must be done or when he is

[4] J. M. Dechanet, *Christian Yoga* (New York: Harper, 1960), p. 178.

already half-asleep. Meditation must never be allowed to become a weight with which we gradually crush ourselves and kill every appetite we have for God or for spiritual things. This would certainly be to "extinguish the Spirit."

The supreme law of meditation and prayer is that there are no strict laws about it at all. "It is very important that no soul which practices prayer, whether little or much, should be subject to undue constraint or limitation," says St. Teresa.[5] There are no successive hoops to jump through or executive examinations to pass so that we can move up to a higher bracket. In the immensely influential *Rosetum* of Mauburnus (1494)—a book that strongly influenced the pious abbot of Montserrat whose spiritual doctrine Ignatius Loyola followed very closely during the early days of his conversion—we find freedom strongly encouraged. Says Mauburnus: "Here then are the steps of the intellect, which are full of abundant possibilities; nevertheless, one must not put his trust in these things, but the sails of the mind

[5] *The Complete Works of St. Teresa of Jesus*, trans. and ed. by E. Allison Peers (London and New York: Sheed and Ward, 1950), "The Interior Castle," Vol. II, p. 208. You may try standing on your head for meditation if you wish. And if this sounds ridiculous, read *Christian Yoga* by J. M. Dechanet. There we read "The whole of Indian Yoga may be summed up in one word: meditation" (p. 47). And ". . . The Pole posture (standing on your head) . . . is highly formative" (p. 150). My point is to stress the notion of freedom, not to parody Father Dechanet's truly important book. I am, in fact, happy to recommend it. Thomas Merton, in his introduction of Dom Denys Rutledge's *In Search of a Yogi* (New York, 1963), calls Dechanet's "a respectable attempt" at using ancient Eastern insights in Christian life. But Rutledge himself sees "no compelling reason" for practicing Yoga. Don Aelred Graham, in *Zen Catholicism*, says Dechanet is "well worth reading," and has long sections discussing Yoga—but without promoting it, it seems, beyond mentioning the special value of the Yoga sitting positions for meditation.

must be unfurled to the winds of grace, and inspiration followed, rather than a set procedure."[6]

Meditation is an art, admittedly, and it is learned the way any art is learned, by methodical practice, step by step. But the performance is also influenced by the free action of the Spirit of God, "who gives testimony to our spirit that we are sons of God" (Rom. 8:16)—that is, the Holy Spirit speaks within us, telling us we are God's sons. When we are inclined to speak to God as his sons, simply and spontaneously, we can drop all the hint-systems and memory devices and follow the Spirit. Father von Balthasar explains it like this:

> The first thing to be observed is the liberty of the children of God. No sort of division [of one's meditation time] may be imposed as necessary or even as specially suitable. At the most, a few suggestions may be made, and even these are to be adopted only so long as they do not hinder the real law of contemplation in its workings—which is the free spirit of God leading the individual along the path of freedom.[7]

> *Rejoice always. Pray without ceasing. In all things give thanks; for this is the will of God in Christ Jesus regarding you all. Do not extinguish the Spirit.* (1 Thess. 5:16–19)

[6] Joannes Mauburnus, *Rosetum exercitiorum spiritualium et sacrarum meditationum,* ed. Leander St. Martin (Douay, 1620), p. 483. Quoted in *The Poetry of Meditation* by Louis L. Martz (New Haven: Yale University Press, 1954), p. 343.

[7] *Prayer,* p. 107.

8 Making Friends

Pray for one another, that you may be saved.
For the unceasing prayer of a just man is of
great avail. (James 5:16)

METHOD: To take time to pray for each member of your
family, each of your friends. Jesus did it, for instance, for
Peter: "I have prayed for thee that thy faith may not fail"
(Luke 22:32). St. Paul did it for his protégé, Timothy: "I
remember thee without ceasing in my prayers night and
day" (2 Tim. 1:3). We can make this a frequent meditation.

When I was still in college, two of my friends took a trip
to St. Louis to visit a friend studying for the priesthood.
The night they arrived in town, it was too late to go out to
the seminary, and so they decided to walk around downtown.
Well past midnight they found themselves on an almost
deserted street, and out of the shadows came a little barefoot
shoeshine boy about five or six years old. He asked where a
certain street was, but my friends, being strangers themselves, couldn't tell him, and he turned away and started on
down the street. They stood there and watched him as he
passed under a dim streetlight and on into the shadows
again. On an impulse they followed the boy, caught up to

him, and talked to him again. His name was Julius. He had
arrived in St. Louis just that day. There was little more he
could tell them. They began to walk along with him.
Through the night, block by block, they retraced with him
all the places he had been that day. Gradually they wound
their way back along all the streets the boy had taken, and
some time near dawn Julius suddenly quickened his steps
and raced into a tumbledown house. He was home.

My friends have never seen Julius since, but they have
not stopped following him. They tell me that to this day they
pray for him. Softheadedness? I don't think so. I'd call it
Christianity, instinctive, grass-roots, Pauline Christianity.
Where but in Christianity is there the faith that men are
linked together as branches of a single sacred vine, as hands
and feet of a single body, a body quickened by a divine
Spirit? Has Julius been the richer for the prayers? Of course.
Was not Peter the richer and safer for Jesus' prayer? Or
Timothy for the prayer of Paul? We can, by simple prayer,
help each other home.

Make a list of those who need your prayers, those to whom
you owe much, people living and dead who have been your
companions on the way and in whose company you will
spend eternity. Make secret friends of all your enemies. Help
the careers of great men whom you will never know in this
life. Repair, through Christ, the damage you may have done
in the past. And lay up for yourself treasures of friendship
in heaven.

The ancient Buddhist scriptures mention a curious meditation method similar to ours,[1] which we may baptize and
adopt if we wish. The aim is to acquire *maitri,* which may

[1] From *Aspects of Buddhism* by Henri de Lubac (New York: Sheed
and Ward, 1954), p. 19.

be translated "loving-kindness" though it is quite different from Christian love and has nothing to do with any eternal salvation, at least not for the orthodox Buddhist. The meditation goes by stages. First, the monk makes three categories: friends, acquaintances, enemies. Then the first and third groups are divided into three groups each, making seven groups in all. In the first step the monk prays for the happiness of his greatest friends. This he finds easy. Next he repeats his prayer for the second group, his second-best friends, trying to maintain the same intensity as in his first prayer. He goes though each group, down to his worst enemies, attempting to raise himself to *maitri* or love for them all. And when this sevenfold meditation has been mastered—done often and successfully—he enlarges his aim and goes on to towns and countries he knows nothing about until he includes all living beings in this one thought of loving-kindness.

There is a good deal to be learned from this as well as several things to beware of. Beware of thinking you can pray for your enemies with the same "intensity" as you pray for your friends, if you take the word intensity to mean emotional intensity. But if you take it to mean, with the same sincerity and real desire, that your enemies be blessed and cared for by God, that they never be made to pay for their sins, that they be forgiven totally as we ourselves hope to be forgiven, the word may stand. Also, keep in mind that the first purpose of praying for people is that *they,* not you, shall benefit. Buddhist monks make this meditation mainly in order to develop their own character.

What is to be learned from the method? Both the mechanical and the psychological techniques. Use them if they interest you. As far as the mechanics go, there is something to be gained by categorizing the people we are going to pray for at times. It helps us think and keeps us thinking. It offers us a series of prayer situations to which we can respond.

But more valuable, I believe, is the psychological effect, a kind of gradual self-enlightenment which results from applying one principle to a series of different cases. We think of people in order to pray for them, in order to help them, and not for any psychological effect it may have on us. But it inevitably has an effect on us. Particularly the people we love the most and those we dislike the most tell us something about ourselves, and by a process that avoids many of the pitfalls of ordinary introspection. Candidly listing a man among our enemies (and why not call them our enemies?— "Love your enemies," said Christ) often brings to light weaknesses in ourselves and areas of our own soul where the word of God has not yet been heard. Once we categorize a man as an "enemy" we are not so easily prey to that self-deception which results in continual mistreatment of someone who falls into that vague category of those I "love but dislike."

The meditative, reflective man can gain political control over at least some of his psychic processes. He cannot command his heart to spring out and embrace an enemy. But in the quiet of meditation and in the presence of God he can examine the tensions between himself and others, and put them within the framework of the truths we have from revelation: that every man is his brother, that no man may be judged, that it is the living God who allows and controls evil, that Christ has taken on himself the iniquity of us all, that as I measure mercy to others it shall be measured to me.

Most people, I think, are sufficiently aware of the danger that in thinking about our enemies, even in praying for them, we may only be increasing our subconscious rejection of them. If this is the case for you, then any kind of praying for enemies that involves thinking about them much or categorizing them is worse than useless. But most people are not this way, and when our enemies suffer at our hands, it is often due to thoughtlessness, unreflectiveness, on our part. Many of us can afford to be a little more thoughtful of them. "Forgive each of you his brother from his heart . . ." certainly implies that we are not well advised to calmly keep a group of people bunched in that category of the "loved but disliked." Air out your psyche. Discuss your deepest hatreds with yourself or—sometimes better—with someone else. Invite the Spirit of God to sweep through your soul and to "make you anew." Meditation time is a good opportunity for this.

Prayer for our enemies is part of every contemplative's field of opportunity, as is prayer for his friends. He aims outside himself, in both cases, but both prayers enrich him inwardly just the same. Thomas More, at one of the most pathetic moments of his life, as he was being tried for treason by his former friends and the companions of his youth, his beloved countrymen, and his heart was all but crushed by their falsehoods and cowardice, made this prayer:

> Almighty God, have mercy on all who bear me evil will and would harm me. Have mercy on their faults and mine together, by such easy, tender, and merciful means as thine infinite wisdom best can devise. Be pleased to amend us and make us saved souls in Heaven together, where we may ever live and love together with thee and thy blessed saints, O glorious Trinity, for the bitter passion of our sweet Savior Christ. Amen.

Praying for friends also is commonly found in the lives of great Christians. Matteo Ricci, living isolated in China, often prayed for his old college friends. He wrote back to his family saying, "One of my best prayers is to think of them." Father Teilhard de Chardin, isolated for twenty years in China, wrote from Tientsin of "the overwhelming tenderness of those specially privileged affections which You have placed in our lives as the most potent created factor of our inward growth." Somehow he found friendship of great power for "inward growth." No doubt his friends were constantly in his prayers.

St. Paul made many personal friends in his missionary travels and prayed for them in particular, as he did for Timothy. And he wanted to be remembered personally in prayer. "Brethren, pray for us, that the word of the Lord may run and be glorified even as among you, and that we may be delivered from troublesome and evil men" (2 Thess. 3:1–2). And to the church at Colossae, in the fourth chapter of his letter he wrote: "Pray for us also, that God may give us an opportunity for the word, to announce the mystery of Christ, . . . that I may openly announce it as I ought to speak" (Vv. 3–4).

Selfishness and loneliness often go together. Selfishness, self-attention, egotism, self-love, prevent us from giving affection to others. And a person who cannot give affection will seldom be loved. He will find the world outside himself rather cold, perhaps hostile, and himself isolated and lonely. To win a friend you have to be a friend: it is the kind of advice we give to the adolescent, but no doubt it stays true for all of life. Even grown men and women can sometimes forget how to *be* a friend. And then they wonder why people seem unfriendly, why everyone treats them quite impersonally. Perhaps their own unreflective self-centeredness is the cause. They have given so little thought to the people around them that they have begun to treat people as things, as objects, instead of as persons, each one a rich human mystery. Even some religious books give you the impression that people are nothing more than "stepping-stones to God." I often wonder what these writers advise when someone objects to being stepped on.

There is a sublime value and loveliness which God puts into people, and he expects that we will love them for it, love them for themselves as the Lord did and as God the Father does. Even creatures below the level of man have an inwardness and beauty-in-themselves which we may not overlook or "step on." Much more in the case of human beings, or our fellow sons and daughters of God: our love must go out to them personally. Only then can we find God in them.

That is the reason why prayers for particular individuals, for their particular needs and desires, are valuable and even obligatory. One of the church's leading moral theologians, Father Bernard Häring, says that we have a very serious obligation to pray for those close to us when they are in special need.[2] But that is still a minimum rule, and barely carries us away from the edge of condemnation. The full Christian ideal is wholehearted love, and what better way is there to foster this love and express it than by prayers offered for our friends and family personally, one by one?

"Brotherly love makes contemplation absorbing and fruitful," says Father von Balthasar. "A man will suddenly become aware that he is beginning to know himself in new surroundings."[3]

When Jesus looked around the supper room at his Twelve and said (John 15:15), "No longer do I call you servants . . .

2 *The Law of Christ* (Westminster: Newman, 1963), Vol. II, p. 265.
3 *Prayer*, p. 173.

but I have called you friends," he was not pretending. They had taken hold of his heart. He did not try to hide it. In that last talk at the supper, his good-bye to his friends, he addressed them, "Little children. . . ." Surely they felt the rough-and-ready masculine affection in words like those. Weatherbeaten old Peter heard the words, and I wonder if it did not have him near tears. We know from the passion account that he could cry.

Jesus went on: "Little children, love one another: that as I have loved you, you also love one another" (John 13:33). "Greater love than this no one has. . . ." (John 13:13). He really loved them, that rough group of men who had given up everything to follow him. There was no pretending in it.

Still, Jesus, we know, could see into the depths of things. He could not take a gift and ignore the giver. He could not look at a creature without thinking of its creator. In every lovable person he met, he saw his Father's lovableness, his Father's winningness and beauty. Jesus was not tempted to overlook the people themselves, or pass over them hurriedly. He really loved them—and for their own sake, that is, because they were good people and were his friends.

And yet behind it all he could see that overwhelming ocean of his Father's beauty and feel the attraction of an eternal and infinite person. In the same winning ways that drew him to his mother or to Peter or to John, he could see the winning ways of his Father. Each person was a work done by God, and, as Jesus explained, "The Father loves the Son and shows him all that he himself does" (John 5:20).

So, in this method of meditation, we imitate Jesus. We try to model our outlook on his. We think of our best friends or perhaps someone we admire from a distance. A photo may help, or a letter from them, or maybe a list of their names on a white piece of paper before us. We recall their goodness and winningness and we love them for it. Then we reflect on the fact that this human person also shows us the winningness of Father, Son and Spirit, the winningness of God.

To clarify: when we listen to excellent music, what is it that we are actually hearing? That is, where does all this beauty and power and clarity come from? Ultimately from some man, the composer. It is just an expression of his, like the look on his face or words from his lips. It is himself, spread over pages of score and filling every corner of the room—beauty once inside the man and now stretched out for us all to enjoy. Bespectacled, deaf, crotchety old Ludwig van Beethoven, with his classical symphonies, has won the love of people all over the world for more than a century and a half, and his cult is still growing.

But when we hear Beethoven's music, we all have the feeling that we are giving our affection to something greater than that little old man. Indeed we are. We are loving all the sounds and emotions of the world which have passed through the composer and which he has re-created and reconstructed for us. We admire Beethoven, but go beyond him.

In a similar way, we may pass through all our friends to God in our moments of reflectiveness. It will not take us away from them. It will only make them more dear, and make us more worthy of them. But it will also show us hints of God more powerful than we can find in any other place.

> *Pray for one another, that you may be saved. For the unceasing prayer of a just man is of great avail.* (James 5:16)

9 Making a List

Let your petitions be made known to God
(Phil. 4:6).

METHOD: To draw up a list of the things we request from God at this moment. We know by faith that we are dependent on God for every single thing we use in this world, from the stimulation of our heart, second by second, to that last and best gift, eternal happiness. In our mind all these needs are a kind of lump-sum request. Occasionally itemize the requisition. It will startle you.

It was not until the civil rights demonstrations started in Montgomery, Selma, and Birmingham that even the Negroes themselves began to realize how bad their social situation was. They had grown so accustomed to their needs, that only a small percentage of their twenty million citizens could be convinced the demonstrations were worth the trouble. Americans at large certainly had no appreciation of the seriousness of this wound on the nation's body until the swelling began.

We need God. We need first his grace, then his care in a thousand ways. God is not unjust to us, of course, the way America has been unjust to its colored citizens. But the peculiar dynamism of an open demonstration of need has a way of deepening our realization of need. Poverty impresses you when you begin to put out your hand.

Our absolute poverty as regards God, our total dependence on him, will impress us if we will just sit down a minute and think out, in some detail, what we must have every day from God: sausage for supper, milk for breakfast, bread and wine, fresh air, bright sunshine; the blessing of sleep, rest from anxiety; patience should we be insulted, mercy should we grow angry—to know the mind of Christ, the fellowship of his sufferings, the power of his resurrection. Each man's list will be different, and longer or shorter depending on his temperament and the urgings of the Spirit. Some will find a pencil or typewriter useful in helping them to concentrate. A visual thing is far more impressive than just a passing thought.

Once our list is made, we may seek the face and presence of God. In the name of the Son, and in union with the Spirit, we then let our "petitions be made known to God." We wish our simple petitions to be a form of worship, of prayer. But at the same time there will grow within us not just a knowledge of our needs. Within us will be a new assent, what Newman referred to as not merely a notional but a *real* assent, that God is, in fact, God.

If we begin with a lowly attitude toward the work of making the list, if we modestly ask God to guide our hand and our mind, we will find that the Spirit within us may help us with the work. "The Spirit helps our weakness. For we do not know what we should pray for as we ought, but the Spirit himself pleads for us with unutterable groanings." (Rom. 8:26) The Spirit knows. And sometimes we will discover as we expand the list that our mind is moving forward toward ideas we have not thought of for a long time. Perhaps we have never thought of them before. And down at the bottom of the list may come items that surprise us. "Why didn't I put that first?" we will ask ourselves. "How could I have been so short-sighted, so narrow?" The answer may entirely escape us that day or the next, at least any half-satisfactory answer. But slowly, perhaps, we will feel the word of God, small as the mustard seed, begin to grow in us. We will sense the work of God in us and indirectly, obliquely, get a slight glimpse of our true selves: that we are nothing, just a void and an empty vessel apart from God.

We "live in the Spirit," St. Paul tells us in the Epistle to the Galatians: we are "led by the Spirit," we "walk in the Spirit." And certainly we pray in the Spirit. "The Spirit himself gives testimony to our spirit that we are sons of God" (Rom. 8:16) and "because you are sons, God has sent the Spirit of his Son into our hearts, crying, 'Abba! Father!'" (Gal. 4:6). "Abba," which is also used by St. Paul in Romans 8:15, is the same word which St. Mark uses in quoting our Lord's Gethsemani prayer to his Father: "Abba, Father, all things are possible to thee" (Mark 14:36).[1] If we wonder whether we may talk to God simply or not, we need no more instruction than this. For "Abba" was the form Aramaic-speaking children used in addressing their father and is just one step up from the diminutive form used by very small children, "ai" or "a."[2] "Abba" also seems to have been the form our Lord used in teaching his disciples to pray, when he taught them the Our Father.[3]

[1] Heinz Schurmann, *Praying with Christ* (New York: Herder and Herder, 1964), p. 9.

[2] *Ibid.*, p. 113.

[3] *Ibid.*, p. 11.

And when we come to the end of our list of petitions, or after using this method a number of times, we will appreciate much more that first and most fundamental Christian prayer. The Our Father contains, at least in seed form, all the petitions we could think up to offer to God: may God be worshiped and honored, may his kingdom succeed on earth and in heaven, may all men give obedience to his word and his will; may we all have bread to eat and the necessities of life; may we be forgiven our cruelties and dishonesties and pretensions—all our debts;[4] may we all be delivered from troubles and dangers of every kind.

The Our Father, full of the most profound of Christian truths, has a form that is simple and childlike, but it is not the less profitable for that. We sometimes may get the impression that any form of contemplation that is "discursive" —which involves a number of different thoughts and allows the mind to wander freely among new ideas—is a prayer only for beginners. It is not so. "The Spirit breathes where he will," even in this matter. We may find simple discursive methods of prayer helpful, no matter how "advanced" we are. There is no way of predicting the way God will take us. Father von Balthasar puts it this way: "We must avoid the impression that discursiveness is a kind of original defect incurred by the reason (according to Greek philosophy), and that progress in contemplation is to be measured primarily by the degree in which it is overcome."[5] We must allow the Spirit to have his way with us. And the Spirit expects us to pray as we can, not as we can't.

Nor should we make the mistake C. S. Lewis warns us

---

[4] "This is no doubt why Jesus so often spoke of 'indebtedness' in his parables. The Greek rendering of his original Aramaic term as *debt*, instead of *sin*, has preserved the correct meaning." *Ibid.*, p. 68.

[5] *Prayer*, p. 198.

about, that of thinking we can always do what we can do sometimes.[6] Sometimes we may be able to pray without words, for instance. At other times our way to God may lie in covering a page of paper with a simple list of petitions and then, with simplicity and trust, slipping them under our Father's door. This may be especially applicable when we have been knocking for some time, and there seems to be no one answering the door. I mean, of course, when prayer is difficult. In speaking of prayer, St. Teresa says:

> If the King makes no sign of listening or of seeing us, there is no need to stand inert, like a dolt, which the soul would resemble if it continued inactive. In this case its dryness would greatly increase, and the imagination would be made more restless than before. . . . Our Lord wishes us at such a time to offer him our petitions and to place ourselves in his presence; he knows what is best for us.[7]

Listing our needs is such a plain and commonplace form of meditation that it requires almost no explanation. People quite naturally ask God for the things they need. In fact they are often criticized for making it almost their only form of prayer. "You only pray when you need something," say the critics. But the new dimension here is that we ask for many things we know very well we will have even if we don't pray. And the reason we do so is that we may

---

[6] *Letters to Malcolm: Chiefly on Prayer* (New York: Harcourt, 1964), *passim.*

[7] *The Interior Castle,* trans. by a Benedictine of Stanbrook (New York: Benziger, 1921), p. 110.

approach him more properly, adore him more as he deserves, reminding ourselves of his generosity, and trying to appreciate how much we depend on him. And while it is true that God will give us many of these things without prayer, it is fitting that occasionally we admit to him our need.

The beauty of this form of prayer is that we often find it within our power when every other form of meditation fails. When we are sick, or preoccupied, or "in a mood," or when we experience what the spiritual writers call "dryness" in prayer—when we seem to have forgotten everything we ever learned about how to pray and can't even think of any way to get interested in it again—we may resort to this and find it works.

Ordinarily the most difficult thing about prayer, for laymen, religious, and clergy alike, is, I believe, to decide to pray, to decide to take the time, to decide to face the Unknown, Invisible God, to act on what we believe to be the true state of things while appearances, and often our own feelings, are against us. To study religion or theology is not so hard, where God is in the third person, a "Him," almost an "It." Contemplation is different, where God is "Thou." It is not so much a desert journey where we have nothing to go by. We have revelation and all the creatures in the world to go by. But the journey is still in a cloud, and God eludes us time after time.[8]

---

[8] "Let us remember this: God does not offer himself to our finite beings as a thing all complete and ready to be embraced. For us he is eternal discovery and eternal growth. The more we think we understand him, the more he reveals himself as otherwise. The more we think we hold him, the further he withdraws, drawing us into the depths of himself." *The Divine Milieu*, p. 139.

Prayer is often difficult, then; irksome, if you will. But
let us not exaggerate the difficulty. In books of prayer one
sometimes gets the impression that feelings of boredom or
distractedness or dryness or lack of interest in prayer are
a trial sent by God to be endured more or less stoically,
one which will lead us eventually to a higher form of prayer.
This is not the answer of Father von Balthasar:

> Dryness should not be accepted in principle as a pen-
> ance or trial imposed on us, but as a normal, everyday
> aspect of love. . . . There is nothing alarming about
> dryness in contemplation; on the contrary, it is reassur-
> ing. Love does not succumb to the routine of daily
> work, but makes use of a hundred imaginative ways to
> transfigure and revivify it. . . . Fatigue, satiety, discour-
> agement and distaste, come solely from man and, as
> God holds in readiness all that is needed to give him
> fresh vigor and life under his burden, he has no cause
> for complaint. His part is to bestir himself and shake off
> what weighs and drags him down, and, having got rid
> of it, start once again.[9]

We are not, then, supposed simply to endure bravely and
wait for a higher form of prayer to swoop down on us. We
are to "make use of a hundred imaginative ways to trans-
figure and revivify" our love. The contemplative is to "be-
stir himself and shake off what weighs and drags him down."
Dryness and boredom and uninterestedness are invitations
from the Holy Spirit to change what we are doing, to find
some other form or method of spending time with God.

[9] *Prayer,* p. 112.

They are not trials unique to prayer, and they should not be accepted as particularly good signs of anything.

And they are usually not purgations preparing us for mysticism. It is not prayer itself—the raising of our mind and heart to God—which we can expect to be purgative. What is known as "mystical purgation" comes about, as I understand it, through the discoveries and lights and mysteries and experiences of contemplation. Father von Balthasar comments:

> So long as we are subject to the law of sin, this fulfillment [of ourselves by God's Word] will always have a painful aspect. We have to renounce what is our own, since this encumbers the space in us to which God's Word lays claim.[10]

It is this sort of painful realization of our distance from God, or the painful knowledge that much of mankind is not fully sharing Christ's redemption, which may prepare us for greater intimacy with God.

The humorist our parents knew as "Mister Dooley" once said that it didn't much matter what a boy studied as long as he didn't like it. The point about school is clear, but some take the same attitude toward prayer: it's only good if it hurts. Prayer may sometimes be irksome, but not more irksome than the rest of life's tasks. It is a normal human activity, but the most challenging normal human activity because it puts a man at his best, and demands that he assume his supreme function as a man. Even assuming the grace of God, prayer still requires more than grit

[10] *Prayer,* p. 21.

and perseverance. It requires the full use of a man's powers, including at times the full power of his imagination and ingenuity, to "shake off what weighs him down and start once again."

If in the past we have tried to give some time every day to meditation and contemplation, and if somehow we have lost our way, if we have perhaps given up meditation as a lost cause because "it is a waste of time and nothing happens," then simplicity and common sense and such plain methods as the one proposed here—which is no more than an imitation of the Our Father—must come to the rescue.

> *Let your petitions be made known to God* (Phil. 4:6).

10 Contemplating the Church

I am the vine, you are the branches (John 15:5).

METHOD: To contemplate the Church. Survey what is going on today and this week, what the Pilgrim People of God are doing: in the homes and on the streets, in shops and offices, editors, college students, priests and bishops, nuns, mothers and fathers of families, rich and poor, old and young, hidden or prominent, sinful and saintly. Christ together with his mystical body, the whole Vine of God with its branches and fruit, are something we believe in and commit ourselves to. The purpose of the visible Church is precisely to make visible and convincing and approachable the love of Jesus Christ who is no longer visible or humanly approachable. We will see in the Church almost every part of his mysterious life "continued."

As the second session of the recent Vatican Council came to an end, in early winter, 1963, the Church's prophets had, for the moment, lost heart. The newspapers said the second session had been "stormy and fruitless." The key issue of collegiality was under fire. Religious liberty, by the new pope's own determination, was put off to a later final decision. The debates on ecumenism had been inconclusive. A magnificent decree on the liturgy was promulgated, but along with it a feeble document on mass communications which Edward Duff called "a retreat from *Pacem in Terris.*"

World Methodist Bishop Fred Pierce Corson spent a half hour talking to the pope, and it lightened up the news. Then the pope announced that he would personally make a pilgrimage to the Holy Land. In the little town of Lwow on the Polish-Russian border three secret convents of Christian nuns were discovered and the nuns imprisoned. In America, a five-hundred-page study, *Marriage Questions,* by John Ford and Gerald Kelly, was released by Newman Press. In Rome, Otto Preminger, producer of *The Moon is Blue,* was decorated by the Knights of the Order of the Holy Sepulchre with the order's highest award for his production of *The Cardinal.* And three great Christians passed away: the prolific scholar and writer, C. S. Lewis, the dignified champion of civil rights, Father John LaFarge, and, by assassination, President John F. Kennedy.

A few ripples, these events, on the crust of the great bread whose leaven is the Church. In the heart of the loaf the leaven worked secretly: the Christian faithfulness of husbands and wives, the patience of the sick, the energy and honesty of Christian lawyers, policemen, nurses, teamsters; the grinding industriousness of theologians, the matter-of-fact chastity of religious brothers, sisters and priests, the mellow optimism of the aged, the ebullience of the young. Holiness, grace, generosity, dedication, faith, humility in rich measure. And yet in each man, the "body of sin," the wrestling with Principalities and Powers, the power of darkness.

If with the eyes of faith and "led by the Spirit" we view all this, we will see that in one important sense, Christ has not entirely left the world. On one street sin has covered his face with spittle and mud. But on another his face is like the sun and his clothes bright as snow. It is the same Christ. It is the Lord.

Look again, and take in the dimension of the past. There in the lump of history is Augustine, Benedict, Bernard, Aquinas, and hundreds and thousands of hidden people, martyrs and volunteers and monks and slaves, scholars "crucified to their pens," parents dedicated to their families; men ransoming prisoners with their own bodies, healing others at the cost of their own health, preaching a wisdom of peace and hope to men who might kill them for it. Yet at the very same time in the hearts of most Christians lurk a kind of cowardice, a fear of faith, a clownish vanity and egotism, a gift for hypocrisy. And in some, seven devils.

But scandals in Christian history, among so-called Christian nations or in the lives of certain well-known individuals, cannot be *because* of their Christianity. Examine the doctrine of Christ: no pretense, no superstition, no hatred, not an inhumane element in it. But it demands much, and Christians high and low have often not accepted it. Still, many have accepted it, and the results among nations and groups and in individual lives, balanced against the scandals, have been startlingly good. Startlingly good for those with eyes to see. What we see is the work of grace going on through history and ever increasing. It all flows from the Church and is the Church. In this continuing visible wonder we can see Christ, still at work in the world but only visible to the eyes of those who believe in the Church, those who have "learned to believe." It would be arrogant to suggest that it is easy to see. We believe, in fact, that it is impossible to see without the gift of faith which comes from God.

This method of meditation, then, suggests that we observe Christ, watch him, in all that is visible in the Church, what is happening today and tomorrow and all that happened since the beginning. On a Good Friday afternoon, we can contemplate Christ in the silence of packed downtown churches and in the long, all-day lines of penitents; on an Easter midnight vigil, in the chorus of "I do believe" of the newly baptized, in the resurrection song of a hundred adult first communicants; on a Christmas morning, in the carolled welcome to the Gift of God sung by old and young together. He is visible in every tiny passing act of hospitality and in the age-long dedication it takes to build national shrines or write encyclopedias. He is in the white-clad nun, masked and gloved, handing instruments to a surgeon, in a leper making the Stations of the Cross, in a young candidate for the United States presidency witnessing to his faith before a congress of Protestant ministers. Magazines like *America* and *Commonweal* and *The Critic,* Catholic newspapers like the *National Catholic Reporter* or the *St. Louis Review,* picture stories of missionary work or of scholarly research going on in Rome, books of history and good biographies of saints: all are part of the great sign of Christ's presence which is the Church. Every class of Christian, every category of virtue or heroism, every apostolate or vocation, every piece of "Catholic news," can enter our prayer.

The theory of all this, the theology of it, was worked out by a large number of thinkers and writers over the years preceding the Second Vatican Council, though its roots lie in the Bible and the Church Fathers. The main fruit of their theological work is the council's *Constitution on the Church,* promulgated at the close of the council's third session. The opening words of that *Constitution* betray its indebtedness to this theological outlook: "Since the Church is in Christ like a sacrament or as a sign. . . . , it desires now to unfold more fully . . . its own inner nature and universal mission."[1] In other words the Sign is eager to signify, to unfold more fully its significance.

The most important book on this subject came out in Dutch in 1960, the work of Dominican theologian Edward Schillebeeckx. The book became available in English under the title of *Christ the Sacrament of the Encounter with God.*[2] The book's title is, I believe, deliberately complex and compendious since it is meant to contain the core thought of the whole book. If we understand the title, we have a start on the theology.

One of the things Christ thought to be his mission on earth was this: to make the kindness and love of God for men to be the sort of thing people could see and feel. He himself wanted to be the instrument or sign or "sacrament" of God, by which God could palpably and tangibly be seen and known. Similarly—and by way of "continuation," we might say—the Catholic Church recognizes its mission to be the task of making the kindness and love which Christ had for men visible and tangible, even though Christ is no longer on earth. The Church wants to be, and is, an instrument or "sacrament" of Christ, in the same way that Christ was an instrument or sacrament of God. The Church through the ages does the work of Christ, and thus con-

---

[1] *Op. cit.,* No. 1. The *Constitution on the Church* is probably the most important document of the council.

[2] New York: Sheed and Ward, 1963.

tinues to make the invisible Christ visible, just as the visible Christ made the invisible God visible. The Church stands for, and acts for, and reveals, Christ; just as Christ stood for, and acted for, and revealed, God.

The two great "primordial" sacraments are Christ and the Church. The seven sacraments we are familiar with are considered to be the "main actions" of the Church, and since the Church is just a sacrament of Christ, the seven sacraments are the main actions of Christ. "When a man baptizes, it is really Christ Himself who baptizes."[3] It is usually in baptism that a child first encounters the Church. Baptism is the first sacrament of the encounter with Christ.[4] And Christ is the sacrament of the encounter with God.[5] Thus in baptism I encounter, I meet, God.

Baptism, confirmation, marriage or holy orders, anointing of the sick—by these sacraments Christ, through the Church, reaches out and touches us at the crucial moments of our lives. With penance and Eucharist he touches us often, for our spirit's health and strength and the knitting together of the people of God. He comes into contact with us through the sacraments just as he might have touched us and healed

---

[3] The Second Vatican Council's *Constitution on the Sacred Liturgy,* No. 7. ". . . The Church's sacraments are not things but encounters of men on earth with the glorified man Jesus by way of a visible form." Schillebeeckx, *op. cit.,* p. 44.

[4] "All the ways in which we may approach Christ—or rather, in which He approaches us—are connected with and flow from this greatest and over-all way-to-Christ, the Church. From the Church flows all that shows us Christ, especially the sacraments." *Ibid.,* p. 101.

[5] "Personally to be approached by the man Jesus was, for his contemporaries, an invitation to a personal encounter with the life-giving God, because that man was the Son of God. Human encounter with Jesus is therefore the sacrament of the encounter with God. . . ." *Ibid.,* p. 15.

us or cheered us up had we met him visibly. Father Schillebeeckx explains it this way:

> If we but think what one human glance, one human
> smile, can do in our lives, how by such a smile we seem
> in a moment to be turned into a new man who in the
> strength of the love which comes to him in that small
> token can begin life anew, apparently with powers that
> were not there before—should we not be able to con-
> ceive how a smile of the man Jesus, God's smile, how
> the God-man's glance at us, can change our whole life?
> And this is what the sacraments are: the God-man's ex-
> pression of love—with all its consequences.[6]

We who, through God's grace, know the Church also
know Christ. We can see him and admire him in his new
People, believe in him and trust him, receive his smile and
his love in a marriage partner, feel his cleansing water on
our heads, hear his words of forgiveness, eat and drink his
pledge and testament of eternal faithfulness.

So remarkable, indeed, is this Church, this new People
called together by God's call to faith, that we are at a loss
to describe it, or even to think about it adequately. One
way we have of describing it is, of course, to say the Church
is Christ. A second way, one much explored by both poets
and theologians, and the one finally turned to by the bishops
in the new *Constitution on the Church,* is to turn for our
imagery to the woman who was his mother, to Mary. For
besides being Christ, the Church *is,* in a poetic sense, another Mary.

The whole eighth section of the *Constitution* expands the

[6] *Ibid.,* p. 78.

notion of Mary "in the mystery of Christ and the Church."
The text says, in part:

> The Church, contemplating [Mary's] hidden sanctity,
> imitating her charity and faithfully fulfilling the
> Father's will, by receiving the word of God in faith be-
> comes herself a mother. By her preaching she brings
> forth to a new and immortal life the sons who are born
> to her in baptism, conceived of the Holy Spirit and
> born of God. . . .[7]

The more clearly we succeed in actually seeing the Church,
the better we will understand the real position in the Church
of the mother of Jesus. And, turning the process around, by
contemplating Mary, we can understand the Church better.
There is a remarkable parallel between her and the Church.
What the whole Church is in macrocosm, she is in micro-
cosm. All that the Church is and all we see the Church
doing, Mary in a parallel way also is and also does.

St. John, in the Apocalypse, pictured the Church as a
great and splendid woman, standing above the world,
crowned with twelve stars, the mother of all grace and
spiritual dignity. Catholics see immediately how this also
applies to Mary. The Church is the refuge of sinners, the
gate of heaven, the ark of the covenant. The Church is the
primary receiver-of-the-Word, which continues to bring
Christ into this world, which fills up what is wanting to
the sufferings of Christ. But these things are true also of
Mary of Nazareth.

---

[7] No. 64. This Mary-Church analogy is explained in detail in Nos.
64 and 65. See also *Prayer*, pp. 23 ff. The analogy is used very frequently by Father von Balthasar.

All these titles and activities are applied to Mary because she is the greatest and first of Christians, intimately associated with the Messiah from the start, and loved and graced by him in a wholly unique way. In Mary grace has had its full effect, even on her body. She has been assumed bodily into heaven. She already enjoys that blessed state of resurrection which the rest of the Church will receive only at the end of time.

On the other hand, by looking at Mary in Scripture and contemplating her, we can discover qualities of the Church which might otherwise remain unappreciated and unnoticed, so hidden are they. The Church, like Mary, is a virgin without spot or blemish, humble, submissive to God, obedient, often misunderstood and misjudged by those who do not yet know her secret or her mystery, many times by good, just men. Like Mary, the Church becomes a mother, is God's perfect worshiper, is actually full of the Holy Spirit; at the end of history the Church will be worthy of Jesus as Mary was from the start, a virgin made fruitful entirely and gratuitously by the initiative of God.

Contemplating the Church, which we suggest in this method of spending time with God, is not so complicated as these explanations. But we will find ourselves with a mystery, an awesome and overwhelming mystery. A writer can attempt no more than to give a few hints of what the Church is. Like boy scouts making a human pyramid, the attempt may give you some idea of what a real pyramid is like and how it is made, even though there is only a wobbly similarity. It is no substitute for a trip to Egypt.

I am the vine, you are the branches (John 15:5).

11 Building a Church

*Let the little children come to me. . . . Of such
is the kingdom of God.* (Mark 10:14)

*METHOD: To put creative talents to work and elaborate
our meditations and expressions of prayer in visual and
spatial forms. Whatever we normally do to express our
praise of God—bows, or genuflections, or sacred chants—are
acts of worship and prayer. Even building a church can be
an act of worship—a prayer. The same principle can work
the other way. How does one pray? Build a cathedral. Or,
on a smaller scale, bow, sing, draw a picture.*

Ninety percent of all learning, we are told, is visual.
People are deeply impressed with what they see and they
find visualized things easy to remember. Perhaps this explains also why many communicative people use their hands
when they talk. Gestures are visual aids. Good teachers are
always drawing pictures. Jesus taught in visual forms both
when he was talking about men and their hidden qualities
("Did you go out in the desert to see a reed shaken by the
wind?") and in describing his Father in heaven ("He makes
his rain to fall on the just and the unjust. . . . Be perfect
then as the Father is perfect").

Contemplation is not the same as learning or studying, of course. Prayer *is* partly study, and, for many people, it is always partly study, and begins in a hearing and study of the word of God in some form or other. Every time we pray, it is because we have heard the word of God, because we have been invited by God to pray. We cannot comprehend or completely understand God's word, but we must understand it to some extent. And that means thinking, study.[1]

So, in justifying visual forms of prayer, part of the explanation lies in the fact that this is often the way we think best. Moreover, if your mind does happen to work best this way, then the absence of this visual element, for instance in a lecture or a book, will lead to boredom and distraction. People who are strongly visually oriented—artistic people—are well known for being often distracted, absent-minded and preoccupied. But once set to a creative task, they can lose themselves completely. Nothing distracts them, not even the pangs of hunger or physical fatigue. Their prayer should be a creative task too. Why not? We are our best selves when we are being creative.

Just to be a bit more clear, the sort of "visual meditations" I mean here are these: to take time in meditation to lay out a scriptural text on a page the way a printer would, then present the work to God; to diagram ideas, like the relationship of ourselves to God or to our work or to the people around us; to figure out symbols that will adequately

[1] This is a delicate point which we should not pass over lightly. In Chapters 14 and 17 we say something more about it. In principle, we do not turn to prayer to become wiser or more knowledgeable. We do not use contemplation as a means toward anything outside itself. Rather, other things are used to take us toward contemplation and toward God. But God's call is a word, and we never leave the intellect behind.

recall some salvific event: the Resurrection, for instance, or the Second Coming; to paint a picture or carve a statue of the Holy Family or of the Christ. Or, we may pray creatively by trying to find symbols in nature or among the objects in our room to help us adopt a prayerful attitude and our worship: the firm mountain, the patient river, the open sky, a letter, a book, a tool.

We may use our hands creatively in prayer, symbolizing by the way we hold them the kind of prayer we wish to make; palms down, for instance, for thanksgiving, palms up for petition, and so on. By way of suggestion, here are five simple gestures of the hands. Taken in order, they can express a meditation method of Chapter 3, an imitation of the Mass.

1. The gesture of begging, palms up. All prayer should begin in an attitude of appeal to God for the grace to pray with an openness to God's word and inspirations. The begging gesture says that. We may add words if we like, or just a single word, or no words at all. In faith and tranquillity we face God. We believe he hears us and sees us. We beg for his grace, and for his Word and his Spirit. We listen. It is the fore-Mass.

2. A gesture of offering ourselves; one hand holds the other, both palms up. Here we have entered the first movement of the Mass, our poorest offering, but our most personal. In it are everything we are and can do, our feelings of shame for our sins, our needs and those of all who are joined to us by the structures of society, our determination to serve, our submission in advance to all God has planned for us. It is the Preparation of the Gifts, the Offertory of the Mass.

3. The same gesture transformed: one hand holds the other with the top hand palm down. We offer to God the

sacrifice of Christ, his life, death, resurrection and ascension, and with Christ all those men through all ages who are joined to him in grace and in the Holy Spirit: the whole Vine, the whole Mystical Body and all that pertains to it. And this includes, in some way, all mankind, from first to last, and with them all creation: all that is meant to return to the Father in Christ. It is the Canon of the Mass.

4. A gesture of union with God: palms inward, one hand holds and "leads" the other. In faith, we allow ourselves to be taken over by God, allow God to have his way with us. We open ourselves to receive the sacrament which is his Word and allow ourselves to be possessed by the Spirit of his Word. The next gesture is a further development of this. . . .

5. A gesture of union with many: we clasp our hands. It is from communion with the Word that communion among people is produced,[2] and the Spirit of the Word that possesses us individually blows freely through the whole of the Church, making it one, one Mystical Body. These last two gestures are the Holy Communion.

I offer the above example with some hesitation. But a picture is worth a thousand words, and an example is a lot better than long explanations. It is no more than an example. The reader may invent his own gestures or avoid the device altogether. But it is worth noting in passing that the common prayer gesture of folding the hands has helped people express themselves prayerfully for at least six thousand years and probably a lot longer.[3]

[2] "Because the bread is one, we, though many, are one body, all of us who partake of the one bread" (1 Cor. 1017).

[3] "In Mesopotamia, the Sumerians, from the fourth millennium B.C., had employed this (folded hands) as their principal gesture when praying to their gods. Cf. A. Parrot, 'Gestes de la prière dans le monde

There is also what might be called a "prayer of the knees," where we have no more to say to God than that gesture of adoration, kneeling. A simple visit to a church is itself a prayer, and often our mere presence there for a while, in an attitude of veneration, is enough. Like the vigil lights, a man's very presence, kneeling in the House of God, symbolizes worship. Visualizations like this can be excellent prayers.

We read that the founder of the Jesuits, Ignatius Loyola, once wrote out all the sayings of Jesus and Mary, those of Jesus in red, those of Mary in blue. This was also the time of his "conversion," when he was first learning prayer and receiving from the Holy Spirit the grace which led to his momentous career for God. It may strike us at first that this was at most an ingenious way for Ignatius to study the Bible or a pious way to while away the time. But I doubt that anyone who knows very much about the life of Ignatius would think it was only this, that the saint did not find his creative visualization of the words of Jesus and Mary as constant invitations to prayer. All his life, Ignatius thought of God under visual images (for instance, as a fountain from which all good things flow), and also under aural images (for instance, as three notes, in harmony, played on an organ).

St. Teresa of Avila warns us that it is not possible, while we are in this mortal flesh, to withdraw our thoughts from all corporeal things and be like the angels. And Father von Balthasar writes:

> [Contemplation] cannot therefore assume a form in

mésopotamien,' in *Hommage à Wilhelm Vischer*, Montpellier, 1960, pp. 177–80." Quoted in Maurice Nédoncelle, *God's Encounter with Man* (New York: Sheed and Ward, 1964), p. 126.

which man truncates his own being, whether for a short
or longer time—for instance, by systematically training
himself to turn from the outer world and attend wholly
to the inner world, or turning from the outer and inner
senses (the imagination) to the pure, "naked" spirit.[4]

Such remarks as the foregoing do not by any means establish
the method of meditation suggested here. But they stress
the importance of understanding man as a single unit of
body and spirit, and that it is this same kind of man who
prays.

It seems to me that some people are led to try to pray
in inhuman or un-human ways. We have seen so many pictures of saints on their knees, apparently motionless for
hours. This may be a fine way to pray for some people, or
perhaps even for everyone on some occasions. But there are
whole cultures, the American Indian, for instance, for whom
kneeling down and motionlessness have nothing sacred about
them at all. And for many individuals in our own culture,
asking them to pray motionlessly for long periods is a cruel
restriction of their whole personality and inclinations. "The
real law of contemplation is the free spirit of God leading the individual along the path of freedom." In private
prayers, a man should feel free—or perhaps even bound—
to act as creatively as he can.

An important thing to keep in mind here is that these
actions are not automatically prayers. We may find drawing
or carving immensely and spontaneously interesting, but
that does not mean that we should begin immediately to
pray this way. Simply labeling the action "for God" is not
quite enough. In order to pray, we must really raise our

[4] *Prayer*, p. 191.

heart and mind and face to God. However, true prayerfulness is not so hard to supply in creative activities because
many of these actions are in themselves expressions of inward affection and conviction and discovery. When con-
verted into prayers by being sincerely directed to God, they
become like the written symbols or sign-gestures that a man
without the gift of speech might use to express his words.

There is no question here of self-entertainment or idle
dreaming. Such pastimes are not acts of prayer. But the possibility remains that we can express—and indeed many
people have a need and an impulse to express—their inward attitudes and convictions and affections outwardly.
These expressions can take many forms, and any form we
may choose is legitimate, provided it truly expresses a prayer
or a desire to pray. Even sacred reading or chants or genuflections or processions are not religious acts of worship by
themselves, simply because they are commanded or recommended by ecclesiastical authorities. We must make them
acts of worship by a movement of our heart and mind toward God.

Exactly how does one go about this meditation? Human
ingenuity led by grace is the best rule. But, for example,
can you do lettering? Take out a piece of paper and a soft
pencil or felt pen, read the Scriptures until you find a
passage that strikes you and then "celebrate it" on paper,
before the gaze of God and for his glory. In your actions
you are saying, through the few minutes it takes to letter
out the text: "The word of God is wonderful. I give
my praise to God."

You may even find it useful not only to visualize, or make
visual, your meditation and your expressions of prayer, but
to make everything about your meditation circumstances

"sacred" in a visible way. It is an instinct found among all primitive peoples and is entirely legitimate—though we would carry it out in a Christian way. Thus we may find it helpful to pray in a sacred place (in a church, for example), and at a sacred time (like dawn, noon, or sunset), taking what we consider a sacred posture, wearing some kind of sacred clothing, using sacred words in a sacred form of recital or chant.

Freedom in these matters is the rule, of course, but freedom is not casualness. As sons of God, we may go to meet him and speak to him with the freedom of sons, but never without filial reverence. The closer the saints have come to God, the stronger their sense of his being and his closeness, the greater has been their reverence and their feeling of a need for material expressions of the sacredness of encountering him. "Religious man's desire to live in the sacred," says Mircea Eliade, "is in fact equivalent to his desire to take up his abode in objective reality, not to let himself be paralyzed by the never-ceasing relativity of purely subjective experiences, to live in a real and effective world, and not in an illusion."[5] Eliade is thinking of such primitive religious practices as building a "sacred space" in the center of the village and orienting the living quarters around it. The primitive man built the "sacred space" in order to shake off the relativity and subjectivity of things all around him, to make his world, which he felt was religious, also visibly religious, outwardly religious. We also may very much need a kind of sacred space where we go to pray and which we reserve for our regular encounters with God.

Many a Christian who wants to pray can be helped by a process of visualization. If we are the kind of people who

[5] *The Sacred and the Profane* (New York: Harper, 1961), p. 24.

can visualize and "spatialize" our ideas and our affections
—and everyone is this way to some extent—then why not
exploit the gift in the contemplative life? It will not always
make prayer easy, but it will help to make it possible.

> *Let the little children come to me. . . . Of such*
> *is the kingdom of God.* (Mark 10:14)

12 Entering Bible Space-Time

*To as many as received him, he gave the power
of becoming sons of God (John 1:12).*

METHOD: To meditate on the scenes of the New Testament. If we call to mind a scene from Othello, we imagine something that never happened. When we picture the death of Napoleon, what we see really happened but is gone, enclosed in the past. But the events of Christ's life in history are also above history because Jesus was an eternal person, God the Son, a person outside space and time. Christ still really approaches through these events.

The single most important subject for Christian meditation must be the events from the life of Christ. Old Testament meditations prepare us for this. All other subjects for meditation are based on this. We may meditate on our work, on the poor, on our friends; we say the Rosary, pray the Mass, contemplate nature: but the center of it all is the Christ of the Gospels, the historical figure, Jesus of Nazareth.[1]

[1] This is everywhere presupposed in von Balthasar. Teilhard also has this view. "The mystical Christ, the universal Christ of St. Paul,

It is valuable to understand why, though here we have another mystery and, strictly speaking, we never "understand" mysteries. They remain dark. But we use what light we have, and we submit to the rest, in faith. Theologians tell us that the historical Jesus, since he was God the Son and a divine person, dwelt in eternity. And God's eternity is not best described as time without beginning or end. More correctly, it denies time, physical motion and space. It refers to existence outside what we know as time and space, or above it, or beyond it.

The great saints of the Church, who were seldom great theologians, have acted on this presumption without attempting an explanation. When they pray over the events of Christ's life, they often assume that the events are present to them. They kneel and listen to the announcement by the angel to Mary that she is to be the mother of the Savior, the Son of the Most High. They hear Mary's reply and join in it themselves. They stand in the temple with Jesus when some cry out, "Thou hast a devil" (John 7:20), but they join their voices to the quiet ones who said, "This is the Christ" (John 7:41). They stand by the cross. They recognize him, risen, in "the Breaking of the Bread." They join the crowds of the Apocalypse singing, "Worthy is the Lamb who was slain to receive power and divinity and riches and wisdom and strength and honor and glory and blessing" (Apoc. 5:12). It is not an imaginary dramatization of something that never

---

has neither meaning nor value in our eyes except as an expansion of the Christ who was born of Mary and who died on the cross. The former essentially draws his fundamental quality of undeniability and concreteness from the latter. However far we may be drawn into the divine spaces opened up to us by Christian mysticism, we never depart from the Jesus of the Gospels." *The Divine Milieu,* p. 117.

happened or of something that happened and is now confined to the past. These events are "eternally actual," in the words of Edward Schillebeeckx. The words "eternally actual" do not explain the mystery. They only attempt to express it. Father von Balthasar expresses the same concept this way: "[Jesus] saw every sinner in this repentant sinner, and in this woman listening at his feet, each one of his hearers. It is God who is speaking, and there is no such thing as remoteness in time. . . . "[2]

Meditating on events of Christ's life has special problems for people who have grown up in the Church. Like children today who rather placidly accept our eventual landing on the moon, "cradle" Catholics may take Christ for granted. And particularly when we are young, we have trouble appreciating Jesus, since we have nothing in our experience to compare him to. If the Christ phenomenon is, in fact, superior to anything else in history, we are forced in the beginning to take this also on faith. We have developed no discernment or judgment. We have not experienced enough of life's bewilderment or mystery to be struck by his saying, "I am the Truth." We have not yet been disappointed enough in the cowardice of human hearts (including our own) to recognize the definitive hero.

For never did man speak as this man spoke. "Before Abraham was, I am." "I have overcome the world." "I am the Way, the Truth and the Life." "What does it profit a man if he gain the whole world and suffer the loss of his soul?" "He who is least among you, he is the greatest. . . ." "Do not fear him who can kill the body and then can do no more." "I am the good shepherd. I lay down my life for my sheep." "This is my body. . . . This is the chalice of my

2 *Prayer*, p. 15.

blood which is poured out for you. Drink, all of you, of this."

Never did man live as this man lived: the great personalities of history, even of very recent history, fade quickly, become dim, and for long periods are entirely forgotten. But Jesus is the daily and hourly inspiration of thousands and tens of thousands. His clearly etched personality divides history like a knife. He lives on as actively as when he was visibly present. Attempts to bury him once and for all have been no more successful than the first attempt. A poor man and a simple man, certainly not an ascetic by oriental standards, but entirely unique, both in the moral perfection of his life and in the demands of his doctrine. As so many writers have pointed out, in him was a perfect balance of those heights of virtue which in most men cancel each other out: divine love and divine fear, devotion to the poor and broken-hearted and reverence for the rich man who is just, the sinless friend of sinners and prostitutes, storming into the temple full of attendants and throwing out the buyers and sellers but walking knowingly into a trap when it was not his but his Father's will. Obedient, chaste, self-forgetting, forgiving, humble; fearless, loyal, zealous, confident, "for the joy set before him, endured a cross, despising shame" (Heb. 12:2).

We cannot get Jesus into a few paragraphs. His complete story, as St. John says, would more than fill the world with books. But day by day, and year by year, the events of his life can become more and more a part of us, present to us, if we meditate on them regularly—and make this our primary meditation subject.

By way of example, let us take several scenes from his life as they are presented in the New Testament. We are occupied with learning to pray. For this purpose, then, let us "enter Bible space-time," the "eternally actual," and see several scenes given us there which bear on prayer. We will take first the Sermon on the Mount as it is given by St. Matthew (chapters 5, 6 and 7), since there the writer gathers together, among other subjects, a good many of our Lord's words on prayer—and it is valuable to have them all in one place in a book like this.

We place ourselves in the crowd. Perhaps we are some two or three hundred. The grass is green, the sky blue, the atmosphere warm and dry. We are poor Galileans, a religious folk, with traditions of dignity we hold to fiercely. Our grandfathers often explained to us that there was a savior to come, that we must keep our religion pure, that our God is the Lord to whom we pray with confidence and awe, whom we approach as a group, with whom our race has a kind of pact or alliance, testified to in the Sacred Books, and we have been promised a Messiah who will make a new alliance with the Lord.

There are fishermen here. They sit together near the speaker. There are shepherds, and their older sons, and farmers, and some men from the town, carpenters, the local doctor, the teachers perhaps. Women and children are here also, sitting together, the babies in their mother's arms, the younger boys and girls hard to control, the more unruly held firmly by the hand and made to keep sitting.

We may go on, filling the scene as it must have been or might have been, to the extent that we are inclined. Then we open the book of St. Matthew and read, perhaps aloud, the three chapters from beginning to end. It is the word of God, and though the crowd may not have recognized the speaker as the Messiah, we do. We accept this word with the same reverence and submission that we accept the Word

in Holy Communion at the end of Mass. We submit to the
mystery.[3]

It is a sermon of some thirty minutes, ranging from what
the speaker thinks of us ordinary, poor folk ("Blessed are
the poor. . . .") to death and the afterlife ("Lay up for your-
selves treasures in heaven. . . ."). But when he speaks about
prayer, we pay special attention. The subject comes up six
times:

> If thou art offering a gift at the altar, and there
> rememberest that thy brother has anything against thee,
> leave thy gift before the altar and go first to be recon-
> ciled to thy brother, and then come and offer thy gift
> (5:23–24).

> You have heard that it was said, "Thou shalt love thy
> neighbor and shalt hate thy enemy." But I say to you,
> love your enemies, do good to those who hate you, and
> pray for those who persecute and calumniate you, so
> that you may be children of your Father in heaven, who
> makes his sun to rise on the good and the evil, and
> sends rain on the just and the unjust. (5:43–45)

> When you pray, you shall not be like the hypocrites,
> who love to pray standing in the synagogues and at the
> street corners, in order that they may be seen by men.
> Amen I say to you, they have received their reward.

[3] "The Church has always venerated the divine Scriptures just as she
venerates the body of the Lord, since, especially in the sacred Liturgy,
she unceasingly receives and offers to the faithful the bread of life
from the table both of God's word and of Christ's body." Vat. II,
Constitution on Divine Revelation, No. 21.

But when thou prayest, go into thy room, and closing the door, pray to thy Father in secret; and thy Father, who sees in secret, will reward thee. (6:5–6)

In praying, do not multiply words, as the Gentiles do; for they think that by saying a great deal, they will be heard. So do not be like them; for your Father knows what you need before you ask him. In this manner therefore shall you pray: "Our Father who art in heaven, hallowed be thy name. Thy kingdom come, thy will be done on earth, as it is in heaven. Give us this day our daily bread. And forgive us our debts, as we also forgive our debtors. And lead us not into temptation, but deliver us from evil." (6:7–13)

Ask and it shall be given you; seek, and you shall find; knock and it shall be opened to you. For everyone who asks, receives; and he who seeks, finds; and to him who knocks, it shall be opened. Or what man is there among you, who, if his son asks him for a loaf, will hand him a stone; or if he asks for a fish, will hand him a serpent? Therefore, if you, evil as you are, know how to give good gifts to your children, how much more will your Father in heaven give good things to those who ask him! (7:7–11)

Not everyone who says to me, "Lord, Lord," shall enter the kingdom of heaven; but he who does the will of my Father in heaven shall enter the kingdom of heaven (7:21).

We hear all this today, of course. The eternal person

who gave these words to the human race is present to each
of us; to me, now, and he presents these words to me. He
comes to *me* personally and individually. He sees me and
speaks to me, instructing me because his Father cares about
me and because he cares about me himself. Since the words
are about prayer, he is inviting me to speak, to speak to him
personally. It is almost unbelievable, really. The Mighty
God, whose silent word of continuous creation holds me
this minute in existence, asks me to speak, to take time right
here and now and say something. And we can't avoid saying
something, because if words won't come, the look on our
face speaks eloquently to him. Words come forth from
the darkness of our hearts too, for to the Lord, "darkness
is not dark" (Ps. 138:12). This is facing God, God with
dark Galilean eyes that will not look away from us until
we reply.

If words fail us, if we don't know the language of God,
Christ helps our weakness. He gives us the "Our Father"
for our main prayer, our group prayer, our Church prayer.
But he fills the gospel pages with other prayers, prayers
people of that time addressed to him and which we can
appropriate: "My Lord and my God." "Lord, I am not
worthy to enter. . . ." "Depart from me, Lord, for I am a
sinful man." "Lord, if thou wilt, thou canst make me clean."
"Lord, I will follow you wherever you go." "Lord, remember me when you enter into your kingdom."

The New Testament is full of such phrases, addressed to
the Lord, and which we can make our own. A single one of
these, understood and said sincerely and often, could change
our lives. There is a sacredness about them that somehow
carries us immediately and directly into the sacred events
of redemption and brings us before the face of God.

An example from the Apocalypse can take us somewhat further. It provides a more complete answer to our need of words to speak to God and to Christ. The Apocalypse is a book much farther from being an ordinary "history" than the gospels. It seems to be an account of a vision or of several visions of St. John the Evangelist. But the book has been recognized and "canonized" by the Church as authentically inspired by God, and is quite instructive for those interested in prayer. We will take only the first major prayer or doxology given in the book, taking all our interpretations of the text from modern biblical scholars.[4]

In chapter four, we follow St. John through the open door of heaven and share in the vision of what he sees there. Once inside heaven's door, we are confronted with a colossal spectacle. In the center, enthroned serenely amid lightning and thunder and the flashing colors of the rainbow, is the Most Holy Trinity, the Father, the Son (the Lamb), and the Holy Spirit with his seven gifts burning like lamps. Near the throne of God are the Great Four, supreme angels full of knowledge and life.

Round about the triple throne are the Twenty-four, the twelve Apostles and the twelve Patriarchs, also seated on thrones, dressed in brilliant white robes, and wearing golden crowns. Thousands of thousands of angels are also present, as well as all the creatures of the earth and sea.

And in this setting, the heavenly prayer to God begins. First the four supreme angels near the throne chant their worship to the Holy Trinity. Their song is itself a trinity of

[4] Some years ago the author did a brief study of the prayers of the Apocalypse: "Opening 'The Closed Book' of the New Testament," *American Ecclesiastical Review*, Vol. CXLIII, No. 1, July 1960, pp. 49–56. More complete documentation is given there.

three-phrased chants, echoing a passage from Isaiah and serving as a model for many of the Church's public prayers:

> Holy, holy, holy,
> the Lord God almighty,
> Who was, and who is, and who is coming.

Then the Twenty-four (the Apostles and Patriarchs) rise from their thrones and bow down to the ground, casting their crowns before God and pray together:

> Worthy art thou, O Lord our God,
> to receive glory and honor and power;
> For thou hast created all things,
> and because of thy will they existed,
> and were created.

Then, at the right hand of God's throne, appears a book containing God's judgments upon his enemies. An angel cries out, asking who can open it and thus bring about its decrees—and God the Son rises and stands in all the glory of his wounds, his wisdom and power clearly manifest. As he takes up the great book, both the Four and the Twenty-four bow down in worship of him, and sing:

> Worthy art thou to take the scroll
>   and to open its seals;
> For thou wast slain, and hast redeemed us for God with
>   thy blood,
>   out of every tribe and tongue and people and nation,

And hast made of them for our God a kingdom and
   priests,
And they shall reign over the earth.

All the thousands of thousands of angels then join the Four
and the Twenty-four in the song. The meaning of this whole
ritual is that Jesus Christ, the Son of God, by opening the
book, will preside over the future, and govern all the things
that happen between the time of his ascension and his return. All the worshipers present recognize the grandeur and
infinite merit of his sacrificial act, and they go on to sing a
song which contains a sacred number of praises, seven:

Worthy is the Lamb who was slain to receive
power and divinity and wisdom and strength
and honor and glory and blessing.

And then all these worshipers are joined by every other
creature in heaven and every creature on the earth and in
the sea, praising equally both the Father and the Son:

To him who sits upon the throne, and to the Lamb,
blessing and honor and glory and dominion
forever and ever.

Then all prostrate themselves around the central throne
while the four supreme angels end the service, singing:

Amen.

Thus ends what is just the first moment of worship in the

Apocalypse. There are many others. From this book, and from all the books of the New Testament, we can learn to pray, as well as from books of the Old Testament. But our fundamental source is, as it has been for the saints, the historical Jesus, who spent real historical time with us. We should regularly spend some time with him.

> *To as many as received him, he gave the power of becoming sons of God* (John 1:12).

13 Unraveling Proverbs

*Every good gift and every perfect gift is from
above, coming down from the Father of Lights*
(James 1:17).

*METHOD: To use proverbs and wise sayings, quotations
and bits of worldly wisdom as starting points for prayer.
Christ is the Truth and the master of all truth. Every truth
points to him, and can lead us to him. Prayer is not the
same thing as study, and religion is not the same thing as
wisdom. But "every good gift . . . is from the Father of
Lights." Real prayer often follows such good gifts.*

Eastern people, of which Jesus was one, live by proverbs
and the ancient sayings of wise men. *Heaven has eyes.
Heaven is just. Heaven blesses the good and punishes the
wicked.* Diplomat-writer John C. H. Wu reports in *Beyond
East and West*[1] that these proverbs were known to everybody
in his generation in China. They were part of the very
atmosphere. Westerners, he says, can hardly imagine how
deeply the ancient Chinese philosophy of suffering—preserved in the form of proverbs—his influenced the Chinese
outlook on life. The most popular poster seen on the walls

[1] New York: Sheed and Ward, 1951.

in China during the last war was: *When you hear of victory, don't be elated. When you hear of defeats, don't be disheartened.* And he adds, "This is the secret magic that has pulled China through so many national crises."

Men have a thousand plans, but Heaven has only one plan. This was also a very popular proverb in China. It is a Confucian proverb, dating back before the time of Christ. Consider for a moment what it says. What Christian cannot see in it a core of wisdom easily applicable to our religion? Our own Old Testament Wisdom Books, written to prepare the Chosen People for Christ's coming, are full of wise sayings. *Bethink thyself of foul weather in fair, of fair weather in foul* (Ecclus. 11:27, Knox)—here, in a text inspired by the Holy Spirit, is almost the same sentiment expressed in the Chinese proverb used on the wartime poster.

The Old Testament, in fact, contains one entire book of Proverbs. Here are more samples as Msgr. Knox translates them:

A fool is ever right to his own thinking; the wise listen to advice (12:15).

Prudence says less than it knows; the fool's heart cannot contain its folly (12:23).

Heart of man must plan his course, but his steps will fall as the Lord guides them (16:9).

Patience is worth more than valour; better a disciplined heart than a stormed city (16:32).

One word of warning in a prudent man's ear does more than a hundred lashes given to a fool (17:10).

Little the fool's wealth avails; he may not buy wisdom if he would (17:16).

When brother helps brother, theirs is the strength of a fortress (18:19).

Jesus himself used proverbs continually, some of which he very likely composed himself:

Sufficient for the day is its own trouble (Matt. 6:34).
No disciple is above his teacher (Matt. 10:24).
Out of the abundance of the heart the mouth speaks (Matt. 12:34).
All that you wish men to do to you, even so, do you also to them (Matt. 7:12).
He who is faithful in a very little thing is faithful also in much (Luke 16:10).
If the salt becomes insipid, what shall you season it with? (Mark 9:49).
Where your treasure is, there also will your heart be (Luke 12:34).
Everyone who commits sin is the slave of sin (John 8:34).

Ancient India loved proverbs, and much of the wisdom of Gautama Buddha is preserved in this form. The following are found in the Buddhist scriptures, and are presumably the sayings of Buddha himself, written down at least as early as 250 B.C.:[2]

Hatred does not cease by hatred at any time; hatred ceases by love—this is an eternal law.

[2] See *The Teachings of the Compassionate Buddha*, ed. by E. A. Burtt (New York: Mentor, 1955), pp. 51–73.

*Well-makers lead the water wherever they like; fletchers
bend the arrow; carpenters bend a log of wood; wise
people fashion themselves.*

*As a solid rock is not shaken by the wind, wise people
waver not amidst blame and praise.*

*Wise people, after they have listened to the laws, be-
come serene, like a deep, smooth, and still lake.*

*The fool who knows his foolishness is wise at least so
far. But a fool who thinks himself wise, he is called a
fool indeed.*

*As rain breaks through an ill-thatched house, passion
will break through an unreflecting mind.*

Simply on the level of proverbs, it is curious to see how
similar are the Judeo-Christian traditions to other traditions.
Karl Rahner speaks of "the anonymous Christianity" in non-
Christian philosophies and claims that "in pagan lands the
grace of Christ has long been operative."[3] Several of the council documents say the same thing, showing that there is certainly a new spirit of openness in the Church to the study of
non-Christian resources.[4]

[3] "The Relation of Philosophy and Theology," *Theology Digest,*
Summer 1964, p. 118. And von Balthasar takes this point of view
also. "Once a man has given his assent to faith in any way at all—
if only in the vague sense of conceding in principle to the truth of
God (or of some Absolute, something divine or all-embracing, a
preponderance over his own personal truth)—such a man assents to
this truth, loves it and hopes in it; he is, either explicitly or implicitly, a hearer of the word." *Prayer,* p. 28.

[4] "The Catholic Church rejects nothing that is true and holy in
these religions [Hinduism, Buddhism, and other non-Christian religions just referred to]. She regards with sincere reverence those ways
of conduct and of life, those precepts and teachings which, though
differing in many aspects from the ones she holds and sets forth, none-

Also the proverbial wisdom of the West—derivative and worldly-wise as much of it is—nevertheless deserves our study, and can also become the doorway to prayer. This kind of wisdom has a curious appeal to us. Busy men who would never think of themselves as intellectuals or contemplatives will have a pet saying framed and hung up on their wall, or have it under the glass on their desk top. There is something gently consonant with human nature in these little bits of wisdom. Perhaps we instinctively feel that wisdom should be simple, uncomplicated, direct, even poetic. Let us look at a few of them a little more closely.

One good deed begets another. It is true, but who lives by it? Can we live by it for an hour? Shallow-minded men will twist the idea into "You help me and I'll help you" —which usually leads nowhere. Christians will see in it the suggestion of a way to set whole spiritual forests growing, will see their good deeds as seeds of a rich harvest for God's kingdom.

God writes straight with crooked lines. It was for want of this insight that St. Peter at first refused to believe that Jesus was going up to Jerusalem to be spat upon, beaten, scourged, and crucified. It was not until the resurrection that Peter understood that God was "writing straight" with the "crooked lines" of suffering and death.

When a deep injury is done to us, we never recover until we forgive. This proverb explains one aspect of the mysterious alchemy of the human personality. But it cannot be dismissed as "mere psychology." A Christian can learn much from such a saying, especially in the light of

---

theless often reflect a ray of that Truth which enlightens all men." Vat. II, *Declaration on the Relation of the Church to Non-Christian Religions,* No. 2.

"forgive, that you may be forgiven," or "forgive us our trespasses as we forgive those who trespass against us."

Money is a good servant but a bad master. It is obviously a fact. But many a Christian lives as though it were not true. Retreats often begin from this very idea—adding a full Christian context. It is Christ who makes mastery of the pleasant things of life both desirable and possible.

There is no limit to the capacity of the dedicated mind. There is much encouragement here for a man beginning a long course of study or research, both of which are very much a part of Christian zeal.

Wise men change their minds; fools, never. The saying has a valuable application, in business, in politics, in human relations. Properly applied to religion, it can help us to remain open and responsive to the action of the Holy Spirit.

A further step along the same line is to meditate on brief quotations from poets and writers. They are easy to find in the standard books of quotations. Christ is "the true light that enlightens every man who comes into the world" (John 1:9). Many a man has spoken of Christ without realizing it. Jesus said, "He that is not against us is for us." And we may thus welcome the wisdom of "outsiders" and profit by the work of the Holy Spirit, even when he is working outside the normal framework of grace that we know as the Catholic Church.

Here is a quotation which may be applied to meditation itself, since meditation includes a process of self-education of both mind and heart. Hazlitt once wrote: "Persons without education certainly do not lack either acuteness or strength of mind, in what concerns themselves or in what is immediately within their observation: but they have no power of abstraction—they see their objects always near, never on the horizon."

Emerson wrote, in "Immortality": "When the Master of the universe has points to carry in his government, he impresses his will in the structure of minds." We need not be distracted by what Emerson meant by the "Master of the universe." We know that true Master, and the quotation gives us a most interesting idea of how God governs the world.

In one book of quotations we find this comment of Francis de Sales: "Do not be troubled by St. Bernard's saying that hell is full of good intentions." Here we have two saints arguing over a proverb. In the same collection we find that Sophocles wrote, in *Oedipus Tyrannus,* "To cast away a virtuous friend, I call as bad as to cast away one's own life." John Lyly wrote, in *Euphues:* "The measure of life is not length, but honesty." Cicero is credited with: "There is, I know not how, in the minds of men, a certain presage, as it were, of a future existence; and this takes the deepest root, and is most discoverable, in the greatest geniuses and most exalted souls."

The late C. S. Lewis, whose books are full of proverbs and quotes from obscure writers, was capable of wonderful sentences: "What does not satisfy when we find it, was not the thing we were desiring" (*Pilgrim's Regress*); "The soul that has once been waked, or stung, or uplifted by the desire of God, will inevitably (I think) awake to the fear of losing Him" (*Letters to Malcolm: Chiefly on Prayer*). And for a last example, here is the Indian Buddhist, Santideva, who lived about 600 A.D.: "All [men] have the same sorrows, the same joys as I, and I must guard them like myself. The body, manifold of parts in its division of members, must be preserved as a whole; and so likewise this manifold universe has its sorrow and its joy in common."

This is a system for the beginning of reflection and

prayer. If we find this kind of thing appealing, there are whole books of quotations and sayings which can become, at least for a time, our meditation books.[5] They cannot take the place of the word of God, but they can be a kind of doorway. Through it and past it we go to approach God.

These sayings will not take us all the way to prayer. They are usually only a kind of philosophy, and our religion is far other than, and far more than, philosophy. "We are philosophers not in word but in act; we do not say great things but do live them." Thus the great bishop St. Cyprian described his Christian flock, which was made up of mostly the poor and uneducated—which pretty well describes the bulk of the Christian Church since the beginning. Our religion is not reducible to a form of wisdom. It is a form of life. There are some philosophers who have made a religion of their own thought. Their religion begins and ends on earth.[6] But the Christian religion is the gift of God. It transcends reason. God makes use of our intelligence—he never requires that we act unreasonably

[5] An excellent collection of proverbs is *The Oxford Dictionary of English Proverbs* compiled by William George Smith, 2nd ed., London, 1948. This volume contains references to many other sources of English proverbs.

[6] Such wisdom is repudiated by St. Paul, though he by no means discredits all secular learning or strivings after the truth. But wisdom which is content with itself, which ends where it begins and leads nowhere, he calls foolishness. "It is written, 'I will destroy the wisdom of the wise'. . . . Has not God turned to foolishness the wisdom of this world?" (1 Cor. 1:19-20) He closes this long section on the subject of wisdom thus: "It is written, 'I will catch the wise in their craftiness.' And again, 'The Lord knows the thoughts of the wise, that they are empty.' Therefore, let no one take pride in men. For all things are yours, whether Paul, or Apollos, or Cephas; or the world or life or death; all things present, or things to come—all are yours, and you are Christ's, and Christ is God's." (1 Cor. 3:19-23)

—but our religion is full of mysteries which cannot be grasped by the man who has only his reasoning power to go by. Only faith convinces us, faith primarily in the person of God himself and commitment to him, then faith in his Son as "the Way, the Truth, and the Life." We follow that Way, believe that Truth, live that Life.

An indispensable accompaniment, then, of our reasoning —when we use these wise sayings and proverbs—is an attitude of prayer, of faith and submission to God. In this way we can hope to pass through these many doors into the authentic Wisdom, Jesus Christ.

> *Every good gift and every perfect gift is from above, coming down from the Father of Lights* (James 1:17).

14 Speaking for the World

I urge therefore, first of all, that supplications, prayers, intercessions and thanksgivings be made for all men (1 Tim. 2:1).

METHOD: To place yourself before the face of God as if you were an official representative for the whole world, or for one continent or one country. It is easy to see that America should be on its knees before God. And it is easier to get down on your knees for America, or for Africa, than it is just for yourself. Kneel then in America's place or in Africa's place. Offer to God the prayers which some country or continent or the whole human race should offer him.

In the half-moon-shaped General Assembly Hall of the United Nations, 116 member nations are now seated. Monday through Friday at 10 a.m., when the Assembly is in session, the 116 men who represent their respective countries come down from their skyscraper offices in the next building and take their seats in the Hall. For each of these men it is hard work, full of heavy responsibilities. Whatever they say in the august gathering is taken as the word of their home government and of the people of their country.

The method of meditation suggested here is that you make yourself something like a representative to the United Nations. You expand your view and assume for the moment that you will be allowed by God to speak for a whole country. Or rather, you try to speak for Christ—who is, after all, vitally concerned with every human heart and mind in every country. You put on the mind of Christ, and you offer to God the Father the worship of his Son. You pray: "Look down on me, Lord, and behold the face of your Christ" (cf. ps. 83, Douay). Then pray as Christ would pray. Or pray in the name of the Church.[1]

Naturally, you may make yourself a representative of any nation or continent you choose, or of the whole world, for that matter. The reason you can do this is that all men (and women and children) are one family under the fatherhood of God. In St. Paul's words, they are, or are meant to be, one body. And there is meant to be one Spirit, one "soul," in this body: the Holy Spirit. Just as one member of a family can be expected to know what the whole family needs, and just one part of a man's body speaks for the whole body, so one Christian may speak for his brothers. St. Paul writes to Bishop Timothy:

> I urge therefore, first of all, that supplications, prayers, intercessions and thanksgivings be made for all men; for kings and for all in high positions . . . This is good and agreeable in the sight of God our Savior,

---

1 "The person who knows himself called has to embolden himself to act the 'role' of the Church (this is what the Fathers of the Church called '*personam Ecclesiae gerere*'). As he can never be this 'person' himself, he must act in the consciousness of performing a purely vicarious service." Balthasar, *Prayer*, p. 78.

who wishes all men to be saved and to come to the
knowledge of the truth. For there is one God; and one
Mediator between God and men, himself man, Christ
Jesus, who gave himself a ranson for all. (1 Tim. 2:1–6)[2]

To expand and develop and keep up this meditation
method, it might be well to make yourself the representative of some people you are actually vitally interested
in. It need not be a whole continent or a foreign nation.
It may be your own family, your own employees, your
own country or the country you are working in or have
special information about. If you are truly bent on praying, on doing something definite and permanent about the
truly big problems of large groups of people,[3] detailed
knowledge of the people you choose to represent will not

---

[2] The very first paragraph of the Introduction of *The Divine Milieu*
leads up to this summary sentence: "It is almost a commonplace today
to find men who, quite naturally and unaffectedly, live in the explicit
consciousness of being an atom or citizen of the universe." Father de
Chardin goes on: "This collective awakening . . . must inevitably
have a profound religious reaction on the mass of mankind." The
council also calls special attention to this: "Among the phenomena of
our times worthy of special mention is the growing and inevitable
sense of solidarity of all peoples. Lay people in their apostolate should
earnestly promote this sense of solidarity and transform it into a sincere
and genuinely fraternal love. Beyond this, lay people should be aware
of international developments, and of the problems and solutions,
both practical and theoretical, relating to this field, particularly those
relating to the developing nations." Vat. II, *Decree on the Apostolate
of the Laity*, No. 14.

[3] "Let all remember that they can reach others and contribute to
the redemption of the world by prayer and public worship, and by
penance and the willing acceptance of life's toils and hardships by
which they are conformed to the suffering Christ." Vat. II, *Decree on
the Apostolate of the Laity*, No. 16.

be a distraction. It will make your prayer richer and more authentic. It is a mistake to think that contemplation can not be concerned with temporal things. Father von Balthasar says: "We must not look on contemplation as concerned exclusively with the eternal, and action with the temporal; that would be to sunder what forms a single unity in Christ, and should become ever more so."[4] In other words, Christ sees the temporal and the eternal together. They point to each other. What happens in time, what men accomplish or suffer or learn or need, matters for eternity. Our eternal life is to be the fruit of a seed planted in this temporal world.

Our prayers for Africa (or any country) may begin with requests offered humbly to God for each of the country's needs; for food, for housing, for peace, for education. In this way, we cooperate with God in the governance of the world, according to the theology of prayer of St. Thomas Aquinas. This is true of all prayers of petition. We ask God for something, and in admitting our need of God, "we take our place in the order that God has willed and thus identify ourselves with his cause, fulfilling one of the conditions willed, foreseen and upheld by him," as Father Yves Congar explains.[5] "Ask and you shall receive," said Jesus. We kneel and ask. We shall receive.

We need not limit ourselves to asking for human necessities, of course. The whole field of prayer can be brought

[4] *Prayer,* p. 85. "Even if he has to forego subjects which appeal to him more and apply himself to things and their implications that have greater objective importance, though uncongenial to his mind, he is by no means the loser; in fact he stands to gain much; for the newly opened-up regions may well turn out to be those he will subsequently most delight to explore and abide in" (p. 73).

[5] *Lay People in the Church* (Westminster: Newman, 1957), p. 89. Congar in this place refers the doctrine to Aquinas.

into play. St. Paul told the Colossians, "[I have been] praying for you unceasingly . . . and asking that you may be
filled with knowledge of his will, in all spiritual wisdom
and understanding" (Col. 1:9). We may also add prayers
of thanksgiving in the name of our adopted country or
the group we choose to represent, as St. Paul did in praying
for the Thessalonians: "We give thanks to God always for
you all" (1 Thess. 1:2).

We may follow the course of the sun, from east to west
in twenty-four steps, choosing the countries or areas we wish
to identify ourselves with, and joining our Christian brothers
and sisters—and all other believers in God there—in prayer.

Here is how one meditative trip might go. We begin by
joining our prayers with the Holy Father. We start praying in the name of Italy, and move gradually westward.
As we go, we keep a general consciousness of all that Christ
wants for these different peoples: the knowledge of himself
and his father and the Holy Spirit, then food, houses, health,
dignity, work, security, and education. Our words, of course,
will be simple, and few. But we will act with a sense of our
world citizenship, of responsibility for all and each. In
Italy there are about fifty million people. We pray in their
name. Then we may move on to these other groups. The
population figures are approximate:

In Germany	70 million
In France	45 million
In Spain	30 million
In England	45 million
In Canada	20 million
In the United States	200 million
In Brazil	70 million

In Argentina	20 million
In Colombia	95 million
In Mexico	36 million
In the Soviet Union	220 million
In Japan	95 million
In Korea	30 million
In the Philippine Islands	28 million
In Australia	10 million
In Indonesia	95 million
In Malaysia	10 million
In Burma	21 million
In China	700 million
In India	440 million
In Pakistan	95 million
In the United Arab Republic	26 million
In all Africa	250 million

An uncomplicated way of extending this meditation is to take up the Book of Psalms. The psalms seem to have the style and flavor of universality. There is something fitting about Africa or Vietnam or my own solitary soul praying: "Deliver me from my enemies, O Lord; to thee have I fled. Teach me to do thy will, for thou art my God. Thy good spirit shall lead me into the right land." (Ps. 142: 9–10, Douay) "Gladden the soul of your servant, for to you, O Lord, I lift up my soul" (Ps. 85:4).

If in this method of prayer we lift up our hearts to God, and if we avoid over-dramatization or any attempt to twist the purpose of the prayer time toward something other than the worship of God and the help of his children, it will be profitable. Sifting through facts in detail and figuring out concrete solutions to world problems does not, normally, carry us in the direction of worship. We must not subordinate contemplation to action. If we have decided to pray, and we take for our book "the book of the world,"[6] then we must read the book in the light of revelation. Ask yourself, "According to what words or actions of Christ should these problems be approached?" Open yourself to the word to see where it has relevance to the human problems you are contemplating.

But far easier would be a simple, repeated word of petition. There are some devils that can only be cast out by prayer and fasting (Matt. 17:20). The Canaanite woman's simple petition, "Lord, help me" (Matt. 15:25) had great effect on Christ. We want to help the millions in this world who, like ourselves, are in dire need of salvation. Let us beg for them. Jesus told a parable in which a poor troublesome widow slowly broke down the resistance of an unjust judge simply by following him around, saying "Do me justice!" "Hear what the unjust judge says," Jesus went on, "and will not God avenge his elect who cry to him day and night? And will he be slow to act in their case? I tell you that he will avenge them quickly." (Luke 18:1–8)

Who is there these days who will speak for the world? Who will cry to him day and night for Indonesia, for India, for China, as Jesus cried out for Peter and as Monica

---

[6] "It may be, indeed it is certain, that it is possible to read the message of Jesus Christ with any clarity and fullness in the book of the world only if it has first been read in the book of the Scriptures. But after that it can and should be read in the book of the world and of man's life as well, so that what is said in the book of the Scriptures may be truly understood; the life of the world, if only it is experienced in its wholeness and without reserve, is itself a part of the spiritual life, and above all in its experience of the world's dire need of salvation." Karl Rahner, *The Christian Commitment*, p. 71.

cried out for Augustine? It only requires love, and hope, and faith—and a wide perspective.

> *I urge therefore, first of all, that supplications, prayers, intercessions and thanksgivings be made for all men* (1 Tim. 2:1).

15 Making a Rosary

Have I been so long a time with you and you have not known me? (John 14:9)

METHOD: To gather new "mysteries" and make a Rosary of our own. No method of prayer has been so successful as the Rosary, where we meditate briefly while reciting a kind of melody of sacred words. But the Rosary skips many mysteries from Christ's public life leaving out all the events from the finding in the temple at age fourteen to the agony in the garden. Many events of Mary's life are missing. None of the mysteries of the New Mary, the Church, are included. We may supply them if we wish.

Saying the Rosary is a serious business. If we take it too lightly, if we say it thoughtlessly, we do not really "say" it at all, for we aren't praying. And yet, if we take a grim intellectual approach to it, its quietness and real value eludes us and eventually we give it up. To try to pray every word with its full meaning, and at the same time to meditate on an event from the Bible, becomes just too much. It becomes like juggling, trying to keep ten or a dozen intellectual balls in the air at once.

Ordinarily, people have no trouble. The mystery is announced and they recall it in a flash. The words begin, and in their hearts they worship God simply and restfully, offering their petitions and their praise through Mary. To do so requires some practice, of course, and some effort and attention. Most people supply their part willingly from the start. And then the method becomes, in the words of Monsignor Guardini, "a quiet hidden land in which we may dwell and find peace, a chapel whose doors are ever open and into which we can take the burdens of our souls."[1]

Once we become familiar with the Bible and with Christian history, we can, if it suits us, expand the method. The origins of the Rosary lie deep in history, but it grew from a need and is someone's invention. Buddhists have a kind of rosary, a circular string of 108 beads on which they recite the name of Buddha. The number 108 stands for the number of "troubles and unpeaceful attitudes." Literary historian Louis Martz records that as late as the middle of the seventeenth century in England there were an immense variety of ways of saying the rosary, even where Dominican influence was strong.[2] One popular kind of rosary was the *corona,* also called the Bridgettine Rosary. The *corona* was a set of 63 beads, according to the supposed years of Mary's life, and arranged in six decades, ending with an Our Father and three Hail Marys. Its meditation subjects were also the mysteries of the lives of Jesus and Mary.[3] The Rosary as we have it today is highly indulgenced, it is

---

[1] *Prayer in Practice,* p. 2.

[2] *The Poetry of Meditation,* p. 101.

[3] *Ibid.,* p. 105. A number of different sets of mysteries were used. Some of Robert Southwell's poetry follows these mysteries very closely. This seems to have been the kind of Rosary most popular in England at that time.

true. But the decrees of indulgence are not meant to limit the ways of prayer.

It is the way we pray the Rosary that matters. It is the method that is valuable and which men have always found appealing. It combines real contact with Christian history with a very quiet and easy and natural way of praying, a melody of words. Prayer and contemplation do not consist essentially in making a speech to God. We may talk to God in our own words, but we may continue our prayer when we run out of words. We may express our worship of him in thousands of ways. God reads the heart. A song, a gesture, a ceremony are forms of human expression, and often enough in such forms of worship we can express what we could never put into words. And that is why when we recite Hail Marys we need not attend to every word. It may be like a song or a hymn to us, expressing what we have no words for or need no words for. We may attend to every word if we like, but we are free. We need only attend to God.

We can, if we wish, include in our rosary of prayers all the mysteries of the life of Mary and Jesus and of the Church. We recall them simply, in a moment, and they give substance to our prayer. At other times we may fill in the details of the mysteries, when we are using some other meditation method. This will be a great gain, and will make our quiet Rosary times more and more meaningful.[4]

We begin with the mysteries in the life of Mary. And

---

[4] The Rosary may be considered a form of "repetition of a contemplation" recommended for people making an Ignatian retreat. Such repetitions are of great importance, and it is almost the universal experience of retreatants that these repetitions are often the most fruitful times of prayer.

we might note in passing an additional reason why we should associate Mary with Jesus: because if we do not, we run the risk of playing down his humanness. The mistake has been made often enough in history, and some parts of the world are still tempted to make it. Without Mary in the picture, we might easily forget that he was (and is) a man like ourselves, who had arms and legs and a body and a head just like ours, whose human face was sometimes lighted up with special interest, sometimes fierce in anger, sometimes turned away in tears. It was a man that the Son of God became. He did not become just the appearance of a man or a divine spirit living inside a human shell. He was not just God wearing a mask. He was a real man.

With Mary at his side we can never forget that humanness, because it was her body that brought him into the world, her breasts that nursed him, her hands that washed his face a thousand times. If he had suddenly appeared out of nowhere, an adult, created by the Divine Power without human birth (which is possible, I suppose), we might doubt that he was a real man. Or we might forget it. But with his mother beside him, we can never forget that he was once a tot, then a boy, then a youth, then an adult who one day left his home to do his life work: a real human man.

Here are some of the main mysteries in the life of Mary, divided according to the way we are accustomed to say the Rosary:

The Early Mysteries: 1. The Immaculate Conception of Mary
                                 2. The Annunciation and Conception of Jesus

3. The Visitation
4. The Birth of Jesus
5. The Presentation in the Temple

The Middle Mysteries:
1. The Finding in the Temple
2. The Hidden Life of Jesus at Nazareth
3. The Departure of Jesus
4. The Wedding at Cana
5. The Visit of Mary to Capharnaum

The Late Mysteries:
1. The Vigil at the Cross
2. The Morning of the Resurrection
3. The Ascension of Jesus
4. The Coming of the Holy Spirit
5. The Assumption

We turn next to a set of mysteries for the public life of Jesus. Our ordinary Rosary skips the whole public life up to the passion, so these mysteries would fit naturally between our Joyful and Sorrowful Mysteries. It is very difficult to make a choice here, and we may substitute any others that appeal to us more.

The Early Mysteries:
1. The Baptism of Jesus
2. The Fast in the Desert
3. The Wedding at Cana

	4. The Cleansing of the Temple
	5. The Death of John the Baptist

The Middle Mysteries:	1. The Choice of the Twelve
	2. The Miracles on the Lake
	3. The Feeding of the Five Thousand
	4. The Promise of the Eucharist
	5. The Confession of Peter

The Late Mysteries:	1. The Transfiguration of Jesus
	2. The Prophecy of his Death and Resurrection
	3. The Feast of Tabernacles
	4. The Raising of Lazarus
	5. The Last Supper

It is well to note here, as we survey this group of Bible events, the special significance of our Lord's divine-human actions. We must remind ourselves that in looking at and considering Jesus as he appears in the New Testament, we have to go beyond what we see. Jesus is the Word of God, or "a Word from God." By telling us that he is God's Word, he indicates that, like any word, he has a meaning beyond himself. The ordinary word "sky," for instance, makes us think of a place. We pass right through the word to its meaning. The word is itself transparent. We see through it.

We are meant to act somewhat the same way when we hear, or encounter, the Word of God. There is something —or rather, Someone—further to pass on to, namely, God the Father; "Jesus" is not an arbitrary and changeable word like the word "sky," used *merely* to signify something else. No, Jesus is himself the Divine Being. And yet he remains the expression or Word of Another. "He who sees me sees the Father," he said. And so, while we meditate on the actions of Christ and learn from him and come to have ever more faith in him, we always are to pass on to the Father. That is what God intends. In the love of Christ, we see the love of his Father. In Christ's power, the Father's power. In Christ's wisdom, the Father's wisdom.

Furthermore, just as the Word of God manifests the Father, so the Holy Spirit of God manifests and makes ever more clear the Word of God, and through the Word, the Father. "But when the Advocate has come, whom I will send you from the Father, the Spirit of Truth who proceeds from the Father, he will bear witness concerning me. . . ." (John 15:26). Where do we find this witnessing of God's Spirit? In the Body of which he is the soul, that is, in the People of God, the Mystical Body of Christ, the Church. Just as we meditate on the mysteries of Jesus' public life, so it is good to pass on and meditate on the mysteries of the Church all through her history, particularly in her saints, where the action of the Spirit is most evident.

We may make, then, a list of saints of our choice, just as we made a list of the public life mysteries. And we may memorize them, in groups of five again if it helps, and use the Rosary method—or any other—in going from one to the other, observing, contemplating quietly the work of the Spirit of God as he has gone about manifesting the Word,[5] the Word that speaks of the Father.

Here are what might be called fifteen mysteries of history, or fifteen great events in the life of the Mystical Christ. There are, of course, numberless others, and the choice of virtues here is quite arbitrary.

The Early Mysteries:	1. Ignatius of Antioch (+107), a saint of courage.
	2. Athanasius (+373), a saint of constancy.
	3. Augustine (+430), a saint of prayer.
	4. Pope Leo I (+461), a saint of Church unity.
	5. Patrick (+461), a saint of zeal.
The Middle Mysteries:	1. Benedict (+550), a saint of monasticism.
	2. Gregory I (+604), a saint of heroic industry.
	3. Columbanus (+615), a saint of foreign missions.
	4. Boniface (+754), a saint of courage.

[5] "[The saints] open up the riches of Christ. He is 'the Light,' simple and at the same time all-embracing: the saints break up this mysterious brilliance like a prism breaking up the white light in the spectrum, allowing first one color to shine and then the other." Romano Guardini, *Prayer in Practice*, p. 188.

5. Odo (+942), a saint of reform.

The Late Mysteries: 1. Pope Leo IX (+1054), a saint of faith.
2. Bernard (+1153), a saint of love.
3. Dominic (+1221), a saint of humility.
4. Francis of Assisi (+1226), a saint of poverty.
5. Thomas Aquinas (+1274), a saint of wisdom.

This list is offered merely as an example, and takes us only as far as the thirteenth century, to the verge of modern times. We may adjust the meditation to our own inclinations and expand it as we will. The man who would meditate regularly on a list like this might hope for many fruits from his work: a sense of history, a patience and understanding of people, a firmness in his convictions—but above all, he should experience an encounter with God the Father, as the Father manifests himself and his continuing Word through the Holy Spirit's patient and all-powerful work.

One of the greatest lessons for today which we can learn from the mysteries of the Church's history is the key importance of prayer. The great men of the Church have invariably been prayerful. And while we may be inclined to diagnose the past ills of the Church in terms of too much of a leaning toward left or right, too much room having been left for the over-liberal and enthusiastic or too much tolerance for the cautious and conservative, still a more fundamental problem is clear: that many, many individual Christians with power and responsibility have been too un-reflective both on the plain meaning of the Holy Scripture and on the plain demands of the contemporary scene. Of course, what has always been in short supply is holiness. But the holiness needed, especially today, is not quite the same thing as piety or asceticism or obedience, but that holiness which grows out of real openness, real enlightenment, followed by real commitment: an intelligent, reflective, contemplative and prayerful holiness. When this is present, we have Mary with us, we have Christ, and we have saints.

> *Have I been so long a time with you and you have not known me?* (John 14:9)

16 Praying Out Loud

Watch, then, praying at all times (Luke 21:36).

METHOD: To pray aloud using the words of set prayers, litanies, psalms or any formula we like. Whether you pray with your own words or someone else's is not of much importance. Jesus on the cross prayed aloud both ways: a set prayer, "My God, my God, why have you forsaken me?" (Ps. 21:2), and a prayer of his own making, "Father, forgive them for they know not what they do." What is important is that you be really praying.

If you have decided to learn how to spend time with God, to teach yourself how, the most important first rule of action for you is this: when you pray, do what seems most sensible and natural for *you*. Books of instruction have their place, but the primary instructor is the Spirit of God who works through your natural talents and inclinations.

God our Father expects us to pray freely. Methods may be proposed to us. If they seem too inflexible or too casual or too far-fetched, they are not for us. A venerable old man once told me that each night as he climbs into bed he says,

"Goodnight, Lord, see you in the morning." That style of prayer suits him perfectly, and I'm sure that God is pleased and perhaps a bit entertained (as I was) with the old man's wonderful prayer.

We always approach God with reverence. We become quiet. We put aside other preoccupations. A rather general rule—which does not always apply—is that we should adopt that position of body which reflects our attitude of mind. We do this in normal human communication. God, quite naturally, expects the same. I know a man who spends his evenings praying in a rocking chair on his porch, restfully communing with God, with body and soul in perfect harmony. Would we suggest that such a man go to his room and kneel? It would ruin his contemplation.

Similarly, when in this method of meditation we suggest that one might speak out loud during his meditation, it is only because that is a man's normal way of speaking. Some people find it helpful to speak very quietly or to move their lips without making any sound. God has no trouble hearing us, and we may find that it is much easier to pray this way. Some people find it almost impossible to pray without moving their lips.

Raising our heart and our face and our mind and our voice to God is a thousand miles from anything like speechmaking. We will get nowhere if we slip into the mistake of thinking of our personal prayers as little orations or panegyrics requiring a continuous flow of idea and words, a turn of eloquence to the phrases, and a kind of artistic wholeness and clarity. "Ah, ah, ah, Lord God behold, I cannot speak, for I am a child": thus the eloquent Jeremias reports his first prayer to God (Jer. 1:6, Douay). And his prayer was heard.

God reads the heart. Sometimes, without deliberately intending it, people pray with groans or sighs or facial expressions of anguish or joy or puzzlement or desire. Or rather, this is the external element of their interior prayers. Normally, however, our prayers do not rise quite so spontaneously. We must usually bring ourselves to pray. Usually even simple prayer is hard enough, even a set formula. But the great advantage of set formulas of prayer is that they help us say what is waiting, as it were, in our heart, but hard to get out.

Some confusion is possible in this matter. One might have the impression that there is a wide gulf separating "mental" from "vocal" prayer, or separating ordinary talking-to-God from "contemplation." The problem is complex, but I believe the crucial facts are these: (1) that there is no prayer at all if we read or recite "prayers" without raising our heart and mind to God, and (2) that there is no higher form of prayer for any man than the kind of prayer God invites him to at the moment.

In *The Interior Castle,* the great master of contemplation, St. Teresa of Avila, lashes out with all her feminine eloquence against what she calls "lip prayers":

If a person does not think Whom he is addressing, and what he is asking for, and who it is that is asking and of Whom he is asking it, I do not consider that he is praying at all even though he be constantly moving his lips. True, it is sometimes possible to pray without paying heed to these things, but that is only because they have been thought about previously; if a man is in the habit of speaking to God's Majesty as he would speak to his slave, and never wonders if he is expressing himself properly, but merely utters the words that come to his lips because he has learned them by heart through constant repetition, I do not call that prayer at all— and God grant no Christian may ever speak to him so![1]

St. Teresa is not condemning prayers said by rote by children, or by people praying aloud together, for these have other justifications, though the heart must always play its part. She is condemning prayer which comes to no more than spinning a prayer wheel and can only be explained as a form of superstition or a kind of pharisaism: lip prayers —honoring God with the lips, but with the heart far away. Our heart is not where we say it is, or wish it were, but where our treasure is. Our heart cannot be in our prayer unless God is somehow present to us and present as a valued being. What stand condemned are certain pagan prayers: "They think that by saying a great deal, they will be heard. So do not be like them; for your Father knows what you need before you ask him" (Matt. 6:7–8). This is what Jesus said just before he taught the vocal prayer we know as the Our Father.

Father von Balthasar explains that vocal and mental prayer go together and help each other:

It is a mistake to regard *oratio* as inferior to *contemplatio,* and to view vocal prayer as primarily for beginners and contemplative prayers as suitable mainly for the advanced. Each depends on the other and presupposes it, and the one should lead directly into the other.[2]

---

[1] *The Complete Works of Saint Teresa of Jesus,* trans. and ed. by E. Allison Peers (London and New York: Sheed and Ward, 1950), Vol. II, p. 204.

[2] *Prayer,* p. 198.

The distinction between vocal and mental prayer, then, is not so very important in practice. In one sense, all prayer is in set formulas, since we can only pray as we are taught to pray by the Spirit, and only in response to God's word to us, and only with the voice of Christ and only in God's language. On the other hand, no two people ever really say the same set formula since we always invest the prayer with our own personality. This gives a unique tone and attitude and significance to the prayer, however "set" the formula may be.

Therefore, for a meditation period we may choose to practice either vocal or mental prayer, set formulas or our own free methods. The latter is often recommended, and rightly so, because it makes it possible for us to be more ourselves. But there is a disadvantage in meditating without the help of a set of words to lean on: that we run the risk of finding ourselves adrift and becalmed, our minds blank and our hearts cold. We may even have the mistaken notion that there is something automatically higher about this state of distraction and blankness—which we usually have brought on ourselves. With a hope that soon we may experience at least a little of the mystical way we may have read about in some saint's biography, we may try to force ourselves doggedly to fill in the time with more of this blankness. Naturally we quickly lose all taste for prayer, are insupportably bored, and perhaps fall asleep. Eventually we quit trying.

Contemplation and spending time with God are not nearly so hard as that, though they are not easy. Boredom and sleepiness are usually a "turn-back sign" given us in the interests of future progress. We must simply change our method. If we combine what we know by faith and what we have learned from common sense, we can pray. We can always pray. We can always bring ourselves before the eyes of God and raise our face to him, show him ourselves, open ourselves to his word. If speaking out loud or quietly in set formulas helps, use it.

This speaking out loud, or at least moving our lips, sometimes helps by giving a kind of kinesthetic support to our efforts to speak to God. There are people whose minds and hearts are most communicative when they have a pencil in their hand. These should try writing their prayer.[3] And there are some who can think best when they are actually talking aloud. We think immediately of the extreme examples, people who speak endlessly without thinking. But there are many others who "think best on their feet." For them, a talking prayer may be best.

In addition, prayer in which the lips and voice enter along with the mind and heart is in one sense more complete, for it is the whole man who adores, and who hopes and who believes. Not only the speaking voice, but, as has been mentioned earlier, many kinds of expressive and communicative gestures may enter our prayer, and may help us sustain it: bowing or prostrating, kneeling, walking, stretching out our arms; or resting, relaxing in an attitude of humility, trust,

---

[3] Louis Bouyer makes this valuable comment on written meditation: "Especially suited to intellectuals, this presents some obvious dangers: there is always the risk of allowing prayer to degenerate into literature. Yet, on the one hand, this risk is not fatal. And on the other, such a practice has the advantage of keeping us from the waking dream in which any meditation risks being lost. The examples of the *Soliloquies* of Augustine and the *Meditative Prayers* of William of St. Thierry suffice to show both the solidity and the richness which this practice can assure to meditation through forcing it to take definite shape." *Introduction to Spirituality* (New York: Desclée, 1961), p. 87.

and dependence. Or singing. One may sing his prayers, even in private. Those who find their prayers dull and monotonous may benefit from reflecting that the great bulk of scriptural prayers, the psalms, are, every one of them, songs.

All methods of prayer overlap. Prayerful people find that the Spirit guides them into a combination of methods, perhaps to one or other method that lasts for a time, or perhaps even a lifetime. Others find their prayer a continual search through seemingly endless dark valleys of the spirit where they can only say, "Ah, ah, ah, Lord God behold, I cannot speak, for I am a child." But even this is prayer.

An interesting commentary on our subject is found in a Korean book of religion written over one thousand years ago, long before any Christian influence reached that land. It contains a fascinating mixture of superstition and truth, but is very much to the point:

> Kuk Je Sa, a famous scholar said: "If you read the 366 verses of the *Sam Il Sin Ko*[4] 30,000 times, you will begin to avoid disasters. If you read them 70,000 times, disease cannot be your enemy. If 100,000 times, you can escape guns and knives. If 300,000 times, animals and birds will be your friends. If 700,000 times, ghosts and humans will fear you. If 1,000,000 times, you will become the teacher of angels and ghost generals. If 3,660,000 times, you can escape pain and sorrow. *But,* you must read it each time with your mind as well as your mouth. Otherwise, even if you read it 100,000,000 times, it will be useless, and, in fact, harmful. Your life will be shortened, you will meet disaster and you will be in a dark place,

---

[4] *Sam Il Sin Ko* is the bible of the Tae Jong Kyo, a native Korean religion.

unable to raise your head. Therefore, be concerned about this, and think of it with diligence."

In finding a good form of prayer for ourselves, we have always to remember this fundamental truth: only the Father can teach the language of prayer. And the only word in that language is the Word which is the Son. And the deepest meaning, we might say, of the Word which the Father teaches and which is the Son is Love, the Holy Spirit. If we are to learn prayer, we must first receive the Holy Spirit, who, in us, will offer the Word to the Father.

All prayer, then, is an act of offering the Word to the Father, under the influence of the Spirit. All prayer in the Church, beginning from the Mass, and all true prayer outside the Church, consists in, first, a reception of God's Spirit by way of the Son, and a reciprocal return to the Father of the same Word of God warmed by the breath of the Spirit within us. Whether our prayer is vocal or mental, our own or someone else's composition, the action of grace is of greatest moment.

The difficulties of prayer may perhaps be traced to a lack of a "felt need" for it. And we have no "felt need" for prayer because we have not taught ourselves the need for prayer. Yes, we've given ourselves reasons, perhaps, made lists of them, and then knelt down to pray. But still we feel nothing. We feel it is useless. Our mind knows the need, but our imagination, our memory, our bodies, our hearts experience, see, know, feel no need. Until we teach these elements too, ultimately until we teach our total self, of our need, praying will seem useless. We feel adequate. What we have for the moment is sufficient and secure. We are not ready for the gospel, for the word which invites us to respond.

Therefore, try as we will to say our vocal prayers sincerely, there is a sense in which it is true to say that only a poor man can pray. Only a desperate man can summon up the energy needed to make the leap up to the level where God is "Thou," make the leap and stay there. It is poverty that pre-evangelizes us to hear and understand the gospel, poverty not only of the flesh but also of the spirit, not only the poverty where the bread I long for is out of my reach though well within my hope, but also the poverty of spirit where opportunities appear on every side, which I can clearly see and almost taste and almost touch. Such poor men can pray. And while we cannot all be poor according to the flesh, we can become poor according to the spirit. We can give our hearts away, to God and to his world, to our family, to our work. It will impoverish us. Then we can pray.

Watch, then, praying at all times (Luke 21:36).

17 Solving Problems

*The kingdom of this world has become the king-
dom of our Lord and of his Christ* (Apoc. 11:15).

*METHOD: To give meditation time to problem-solving. At
the time of the election of a Holy Father for the Church, the
Cardinals are instructed to give themselves to prayer before
they vote. Most of us do not elect popes, but we do elect pres-
idents. The election of our government or the outcome of
many a local referendum is also relevant to the kingdom of
God. We should give ourselves to prayer over such problems.*

Once we have seen that this is God's world and that the
Christian task is to make the world God's kingdom, and that
this is done not by ecclesiastical and sacramental means alone
but also in and through the work of the world, we must conclude that all important human problems may enter the
world of contemplation.[1] We must take time out to look at
our problems in the light of God's revelation. We must learn
to meditate on the Bible and the newspaper side by side, to

[1] "Neither family responsibilities nor any other concerns of secular
life should be extraneous to the conduct of our spiritual lives. . . ."
Vat. II, *Decree on the Apostolate of the Laity,* No. 3.

see how they relate to each other, to help bring them more into contact.

The word of God is given to the world that the world may have life. And this life, while primarily interior and individual, is not entirely so. Grace is also social. Some men reject the word, and life and grace in the world suffer a loss. But others accept the word, accept grace and the grace-life. To as many as receive him, he gives the power to become sons of God (cf: John 1:12). And the sons of God are meant to have some effect on God's world. The Bible, then, God's word, can affect the news. Every Christian citizen must work so that the word of God is ever more and more effective in the world.

The world, on the other hand, influences Christian life and the progress of the kingdom of God by being the field in which that life works. The situations of need and of opportunity which are reported in the newspaper are, from one point of view, occasions of grace. "I stand at the door and knock," says Christ. "What you do (or do not do) for the least of my brethren, you do for me." "All of creation is full of expectancy because it is waiting for the sons of God to be made known," St. Paul tells the Romans. The Christian, more than anyone else, should find the newspaper an important part of his life.

The question here is not: Should Christians bring these worldly problems into their prayer? But rather we ask: Should Christians pray over, meditate on, these problems? To this we answer: decidedly *yes*. He is obliged to it by his Christian responsibility to function effectively and intelligently in society. Father von Balthasar's comment on this is the following:

When he leaves his prayer and comes to his work in the world, he is not blinded by the splendor from above, or unable to find his way about. . . . He comes as one sent, who has received unawares, in contemplation, the full equipment for his task as a Christian, the power as well as the aptitude, and also the taste for it.[2]

If a man's mission from God takes him on most days into the City of Man—to a factory or a classroom or an office, a milieu where the newspaper, the telephone, the journals of opinion, are as life-giving as the air itself, then his prayer life should be relevant to all these things. Prayer for the active Christian should be of the same fabric as his activity. We assume that his activity is God's work.

Prayer should not normally serve as a haven or refuge from work. Prayer is not, of itself, rest, though it may be restful. It may also be disturbing, just as God's work and the problems of God's kingdom can be disturbing. A Christian's prayer must send him right out into his work, as a man sent from God with a mission. And it should light up the way for him.

We do not "stop to pray" the way a man stops to calm himself down or catch his breath. This is far too narrow a view of the matter. For the purpose of relief from tension or catching your breath, a game of golf, a hot shower and an hour's rest would serve better than any amount of praying.

Of course as we may fill in our moments of rest with converse with God, but normally we go to prayer to hear God's word, spoken to us in Scripture, or in our hearts, or in nature —including human nature—and this is where the newspaper

2 *Prayer,* p. 99.

comes in. When that word says, "What you do for the least of my brethren, you do for me" and we see his brethren involved in problems which are in no way simple or easy to solve, then response to that word requires that we face those problems, think prudentially about them, try to come to some intelligent frame of mind and perhaps even to some action—all in the presence of God whose instruments and servants we are in such things.[3]

What are the sorts of problems we must meditate about? We may think of them in two categories: how to heal wounds and how to promote growth. To put it another way, our two problems are how to reduce suffering and how to release the energy in the world by which it can move toward its fulfillment; in scriptural terms, how to apply to death the fruits of the resurrection, and how to open the way to the reign of the Holy Spirit.

In the first group are such problems as these: How to guarantee every human being the freedom he has the right to? How to distribute the world's food to the world's people, most of whom are now without it? How to provide work for able men and women now idle? How to deal with overcrowding and population pressure as it exists now, and as it seems destined to become? How disarm angry nations? How control genocidal weapons? How educate the illiterate masses? How safeguard families and the rights of women and children? How clear the slums? How control disease? How

[3] "Only by the guidance of faith and reflection on the word of God can any man come to recognize in every moment and every place the God 'in whom we live and move and have our being' (Acts 17:28). Only through faith and God's word can we seek out his will in every decision, see Christ in all men, whether friend or stranger, and judge accurately the true value and meaning of secular realities. . . ." Vat. II, *Decree on the Apostolate of the Laity*, No. 4.

provide for refugees, orphans, migrants, the derelict and the insane? How renew the Church and heal divisions among Christians?

Of the second type are problems such as these: How unite mankind? How organize and direct scientific research? How improve agriculture? How promote creativity and coopera- tion? How lengthen human life? How improve communica- tions and travel? How use atomic energy? How see to the fitting worship of God and the spread of the gospel?

There is another category of things we may pray over which spans the preceding two categories: our own judgment of assent or dissent or suspension of agreement with the decisions or judgments of others. There is no real concern of the world which is not also our concern. Far away as some issues may seem, it is important to side with grace even before grace approaches us personally, and to renounce all that is opposed to God even when it appears to be remote or un- related to us. For all the world's successes are our successes, and all the world's evil attacks the body of mankind to which I belong. Hard-core irreverence toward human beings no matter how "venial," dishonesty in public life or in the market place no matter how much it is taken for granted, worship of idols of whatever kind—all these we must reject at least in our hearts.

And occasionally we must reject them in public. For public opinion, as Stuart Chase has observed, is the most powerful force in the world today and an obligation which no adult individual can escape. According to Pius XII:

Public opinion is the attribute of every society made up of men who, conscious of their personal and social be- havior, are closely concerned in the community of which

they are members. . . . In the eyes of every Christian, to
stifle the citizens' voice and force them to be silent is an
outrage of man's natural right. . . . [There must also be
public opinion in the Church.] She is a living body, and
something would be lacking to her life were there no
public opinion in it, a want for which the blame would
rest on pastors and faithful. . . .[4]

But if we are going to voice our opinion in public, it must
certainly be the fruit of reflection and prayer. We must speak
out as much as possible with the voice of Christ and for the
purposes of his kingdom.

Modern Christians who may be attempting for the first
time to become reflective and prayerful in a formal way—
taking time out daily or weekly to spend time with God—
may find this method the best way to begin. If they do so
before the face of God, recalling his governance of the world
and the power of prayer, they will profit a great deal and so
will the world. One layman reported recently in the Catholic

---

[4] Pope Pius XII in an address at the International Congress of the
Catholic Press, Rome, 1950. And Father von Balthasar: "[The Chris-
tian] must make way within himself for a sense of the interests and
needs of the Church as a whole. They may concern him personally
only slightly or interest him only remotely; the subjects to which his
attention is directed will be of importance either for the Church in
general or for someone to whom he may communicate the outcome
later on, in the course of conversation or some other form of contact."
Prayer, p. 73. The Second Vatican Council's *Decree on the Media of
Social Communication*, though it was greeted with justified disappoint-
ment by many American commentators, stresses several times the need
to "support and advance public opinion." "The prompt publication
of affairs and events provides every individual with a fuller, continuing
acquaintance with them, and thus all can contribute more effectively
to the common good. . . ." No. 5. See also No. 8 and No. 12.

press, "The most rewarding evening of recollection I have attended consisted merely of a priest reading aloud news stories from a newspaper and commenting in a reflective way on each article. Since that time, I cannot read the paper without being led into prayer and meditation."

The larger problems of social concern are particularly good material for group discussion since they are so complex. But group discussion and private meditation may be thought of as going well together. The *cursillo* movement acts on this presumption. Meditation may both precede and follow a discussion or a conversation. Or it may happen by chance that a few minutes spent talking to someone will provide matter for later reflection in God's presence. Of course, the whole thing may be done formally, with a group gathering together and then spending some time in private reflection before the conversation is opened, or afterward.

There are several dangers to be avoided in this type of meditation. One is the danger of a kind of romantic secularism which would overemphasize the value of human tasks to the extent that they would have no need of reference to God. It may take the form of a kind of exaggerated optimism which would think that, by human efforts alone, we could bring the world to its fulfillment. Such is not the case. It is Christ who will bring the world to its fulfillment. Without him we can do nothing: but he is with us. We may be optimistic, but it is unrealistic to think that we can overcome death and human malice in this world. Whether our outlook on the future of the world be bright or dim, no one's view can be so bright that he cannot see that the world's way, in imitation of its Redeemer, is a way of the cross—however much we walk "with joy set before us."

We may, and we must, continually improve the social

order. It is the command of God, an advancement of his creation and Incarnation, a condition of our own salvation, and the right of the people affected. It is Christianity's first task in many countries today. But it is not the whole of the gospel. Men must know of the Father and of the Messiah whom he sent. It is sobering to reflect that it was in an ideally structured milieu that Adam rejected God.

Another thing. People do not realize how static their lives are without meditation. Isolationists remain isolated, extremists stay extreme, cynics stay sour. But there is a further requirement. Our meditation itself remains static unless we are open, and willing to deny ourselves. When we meditate on human problems, we have to hold ourselves ready to do whatever God wants. Our frame of mind is to be like Samuel's: "Speak, Lord, and thy servant heareth." We are open. We are ready. Like a chauffeur with perfect trust in his master, we must be ready to go in any direction at all, ready to obey.

This is the frame of mind we need to pray well. Such openness includes much of what is normally meant by the words "detachment from creatures" or "indifference to creatures," provided these phrases are properly understood. Detachment or indifference does not mean that we take an aloof and detached attitude toward the people around us, or that we are indifferent to the books that are being written or the plays that are being broadcast on TV. Nor does it mean that we don't notice or care how food tastes or how lovely the autumn sky may be. The meaning is simply that we are not so unreasonable about golf or bridge that we will let it keep us from serving our family; or so anxious to make a few extra dollars that we will, for instance, sell any kind of books or teach any kind of doctrine. The point here is that, aside from the harm we may do, disorderly attachments can prevent us from praying with any depth. They tend to close us up, to close in our minds and hearts. The Spirit is left with little room to work.

Writers today point out that openness and detachment are ideals carried out differently by people with different responsibilities or careers. Most Christians are busy from day to night with the work of the world. It is God's work because it is God's world. These people cannot in conscience detach themselves from the world's concerns, either on the job or at their prayer. The men who represent them in the government, the honesty of medical advertising in their neighborhood, individuals and groups within reach who are suffering physically or politically or economically, the public image of their church, the obligations and opportunities facing their nation or the whole world community, all of these must concern them. They must be open to them. These matters are in their field of vision as they come to God in prayer.

On the other hand, people who are not busy with the work of the world, especially those priests and religious who live a monastic life of penance and prayer, can and should detach themselves from much of the world's business. It would only interfere with their real work, which is the formal worship of God. Still, they may never allow themselves to lose their respect for the world's work, nor can they be so detached from creatures that they deliberately cease to grow in appreciation for beautiful things: the faces of laughing children, the joy of human friendship, the charm of fertile forests and mountains, the awesome beauty and power discovered by modern science—for these are ways God reveals himself to men. There is hardly any better way to grow in love for Almighty God than to find God lovely. And he reveals himself in all lovely things. For every Christian, there are limits to what he can be detached from.

Still asceticism has its place. Jesus, it is true, was not an ascetic, not an ascetic of the ordinary kind who, like the Baptist, made privation and suffering a fundamental part of his daily life. Still, in the large view of his life, especially in the light of his freely chosen passion and death, he practiced a kind of lifelong or total asceticism. Suffering and death were welcomed as roads to victory and glory. And there certainly was an independence of creatures in his life, a self-direction unaffected by his feelings. He invited his followers, if they wished, to leave home, to give their possessions away, to avoid honors, to prefer poverty and meekness and even sorrow, and to be cautious about wealth and earthly rewards, to care little about clothes or food, to love enemies, to return good for evil, to avoid even interior sins. Openness alone will not accomplish this. There must be a place for self-denial. It is a part of every Christian life, and absolutely necessary for contemplation.

But life itself, a good life, provides much of the asceticism. The good life itself educates us in detachment. Father de Chardin makes much of this:

Anyone whose aim, in conquering the earth, has really been to subject a little more matter to spirit has, surely, begun to take leave of himself at the same time as taking possession of himself. This is also true of the man who rejects mere enjoyment, the line of least resistance, the easy possession of things and ideas, and sets out courageously on the path of work, inward renewal and the ceaseless broadening and purification of his ideal. And it is true, again, of the man who has given his time, his health, or his life to something greater than himself—a family to be supported, a country to be saved, a truth to be discovered, a cause to be defended. All these men are continually passing from attachment to detachment as they faithfully mount the ladder of human endeavour.[5]

Bringing human problems into prayer, or bringing prayer to human problems, sometimes solves the difficulties of both. The kingdom of God is both within us and outside us. But really they are not two kingdoms but one kingdom.

> *The kingdom of this world has become the kingdom of our Lord and of his Christ* (Apoc. 11:15).

[5] *The Divine Milieu*, pp. 97–98.

18 Ransacking the Missal

I will offer the sacrifice of thanksgiving, and I will call upon the name of the Lord (Ps. 115:8).

METHOD: To take for the subject of our meditations the actual text of the Mass. Words or phrases or whole prayers there can be appropriated for use in our private prayer life. Many of the best and most authentic prayers of the Christian ages lie hidden like buried treasure in our missal. And in the heart of it all, the Eucharist.

Learning the art of meditation and prayer, the technique of spending time with God, is not so much like learning a totally new language. It is more like learning to play the piano or violin. It is an art, fundamentally, even though it is also more than an art, since true prayer begins with grace from God and is his gift. But as an art, provided we have a modicum of talent—and for prayer, all of us have —we can eventually learn the art by practice. The art of meditation has its own five-finger exercises and its scales. It demands practice, and it eventually leads to performance, for the glory of God and for our personal and social growth.

Almost everyone who learns the art of playing the piano

eventually accumulates a little group of memorized passages, snips and snatches a few bars long, which become a part of himself. When he finds himself without music, he turns to these. Playing them with ease and relaxation is often the most enjoyable part of knowing how to play the piano.

Similarly, in becoming prayerful Christians, in learning the art of meditation, we do well to accumulate a small number of meaningful phrases and passages from the compositions of others and making them a part of ourselves. The liturgical Mass text constitutes a collection of the most ancient and dependable responses to God of his people through the centuries. For instance, the formula of consecration almost certainly antedates anything in the New Testament.[1] Our "Holy, Holy, Holy" is from the Apocalypse. The prayer "Through him and with him and in him," which is in one sense the climax of the Mass, also comes from the primitive Church. *"Sursum corda: Habemus ad Dominum"* was used in St. Augustine's day. The *Kyrie, eleison,* is from the sixth century.

Not all of these prayers are meant to be said, in the first instance, by the people, of course. Some are written for the priest. A layman can only say them if he enters into the spirit of the ministerial priesthood—which is not so difficult since all share in some way in the priesthood of Christ, ordained to it first by baptism, then by confirmation.[2] To come to understand what these prayers contain and to use them in private will, naturally, increase our ability to take our part

[1] The words of consecration appear four times in the New Testament, but none is exactly the formula used in the Mass.

[2] "Being a participation in the priesthood of the Church, and so of the High Priest, the characters of baptism and confirmation are also an ordination." E. Schillebeeckx, *Christ the Sacrament of the Encounter with God,* p. 167.

in the Mass and enter into its spirit. But this is not the main point of this method of meditation. What is central is this: that we must learn to pray—all day long, at scattered moments, in every circumstance—in a really Christian way. We must learn this art from the masters, or rather in this case from the Master—who taught it to the Church through his Spirit.

Let us take some examples. Perhaps we are the sort of person who makes a daily, or at least an occasional, visit to a church at lunch hour or on our way to work. What better prayer to have ready—memorized and understood—than this: "May what we have taken into our mouths, Lord, be received with sincerity by our souls, so that this gift given to us in time may be for our healing in eternity." It is the first thanksgiving prayer after Holy Communion. The prayer's first mark of special value is that it is in the plural. When you pray it, then, you do so in the name of all the Church or, if you wish, in the name of all who received the sacrament with you that morning. And there could hardly be a more appropriate prayer for a visit to the Blessed Sacrament, a prayer that recalls the reception of the sacrament as food and renews in us the effects of the sacrament: union with God and the Church.

Another example: "Lamb of God, you who take away the world's sins, have mercy on us." We would hardly think of praying this way privately if we did not have the text of the Mass for a guide. Here the Church puts on our lips a prayer right at the heart of the Church's faith. It is addressed to the heavenly Christ, the Lord, whom the Apocalypse pictures for us as appearing like a victorious warrior still marked with his wounds—a Lamb "standing as if slain." We beg his mercy, and in doing so acknowledge his divinity and what is

most divine in him, his mercy. The man who freely allows
the Word of God to form him will become what the Father
wills, another Christ. He will offer himself for the Father to
reveal his Son in him. From this point of view, all of life may
be considered a process of "earning our wounds." Hands
marked by work, feet marked by searching, heart marked by
mercy, the Christian will at the end of his life and forever
resemble Christ, "standing as if slain."

"Through him and with him and in him are given to
you, God the almighty Father, in the unity of the Holy Spirit
all honor and all glory for ever and ever, Amen." Here is an
enthusiastic and triumphant prayer which might come to our
lips at moments of great pleasure, when we wish to enjoy
God's creatures with gratitude and moderation.

"Holy, holy, holy": we learn to pray even in this way.
These are words of adoration, of bowing low, of prostration,
before the terrible and sacred mystery of the Divine Being.
It is perfect prayer for praising God for his visible created
wonders—or in whatever circumstance we may feel inclined
to use it.

But of all the prayers made available to us in the Mass
text, perhaps there is none so surprisingly neglected (though
it stands at the absolute peak of the Mass, and, in fact, at the
peak of our religion) as: "Take this. . . . This is my body. . . .
This is the cup of my blood." We hesitate. Yet we read in
St. Paul: "Offer up your bodies as a living sacrifice, consecrated to God and worthy of his acceptance; this is the
worship due from you as rational creatures" (Rom. 12:1–2,
Knox). Still, out of reverence for the central and most
baffling mystery of our religion, we are slow to make the
words of consecration our own. Yet this, I believe, is the most
fundamental insight in *The Divine Milieu*.

We know the words of consecration are not words to be
said by the people at Mass. They are not even said by the
priest in the name of the people or "in the person of" the
people. They are said by the priest "in the person of Christ"
—when the priest assumes for the moment the person of
Christ and makes present and places upon the altar the
sacrifice which pleases the Father and redeems men.

We read in 1 Cor. 11:26, "As often as you do this [perform
the Eucharist], you proclaim the death of the Lord until he
come." The action of the Eucharistic Sacrifice is, then, a
proclamation, a preaching, a statement, of the word of God.
We must listen to it and try to understand. Though it is a
great mystery, it is nevertheless the central preaching of our
gospel.[3] And it is also our central prayer, said to God by the
priest acting in the person of Christ, but resounding in
harmonics through the whole of our religion. And it is particularly in these "harmonics" that we can appropriate the
words of consecration and make them our own prayer. That
is to say, the ordinary Christian cannot say, "Take this. . . .
This is my Body. . . . This is the cup of my blood" in its
primary meaning, either as the worship which the sacrifice
of Christ offers to the Father in every Mass or as the words
of the sacrament and covenant which Christ re-presents to
the Church at every Mass. But I may offer my own body and
blood "as a living sacrifice, consecrated to God," and in this
case use the sacred words of consecration to express my
prayer. "Lord, here, this is *my* body, this is *my* blood which
is given for you."

---

[3] ". . . The Eucharist is the outstanding means whereby the faithful
may express in their lives and manifest to others the mystery of Christ
and the real nature of the true Church." Vat. II, *Constitution on the
Sacred Liturgy*, No. 1.

We may use these words in other circumstances too. Just as Christ's secondary or harmonic meaning of the sacred words meant, "I hereby give my death and resurrection to all men," we may say the words in imitation of him, and indicate by them: "I too give my life and my death and my resurrection to all men." As Christ meant by the sacred words: "I give you this sacrament so that when I have finally left the world, you will have a visible and available evidence and instrument of my love," so we may recite the words in the meaning: "I offer to men my body and blood as a kind of visible and available sacrament of the invisible Christ."

The words of consecration were a favorite prayer of Father de Chardin. According to *The Divine Milieu*, there is a sense in which each of us should take the matter of the world into our hands and recite over it, in the name of Christ, "This is My Body." Doing so is, in his view, that best way to describe the work of life: to consecrate the world. We take up the matter of the world, everything within our reach: all the time we have to live, all we can know, all the work we can do toward improving the world and all the suffering we must endure both to grow and diminish, all our activities and passivities. Taking all this in our hands, in faith we consecrate it, believing it can all become part of the life of the Mystical Christ. It is our very dedication to daily work in the world that consecrates the world and makes it all come together in a unity in Christ:

In our hands, in the hands of all of us, the world and life (*our world, our life*) are placed like a Host, ready to be charged with the divine influence, that is to say with a real presence of the incarnate Word.[4]

[4] *The Divine Milieu*, p. 136.

. . . in repeating over *our* lives the words the priest
says over the bread and wine before consecration, we
should pray, each one of us, that the world may be
transfigured for our use; *"ut nobis Corpus et Sanguinis
fiat . . . Domini nostri Jesu Christi"* [the Latin words
from the Mass: "so that it become for us the Body and
Blood of Our Lord Jesus Christ"].[5]

As we come to know the Mass prayers better and use them
familiarly ourselves, we will notice an unmistakable "He-
brewness" about them. We must always remember that in
the first days of the Church, most of the Christians were
Jews. They had all celebrated the Passover many times, so
they had relatively little trouble seeing the connection between their ancient Paschal Lamb and Jesus Christ. But there
was this difference. The New Paschal Lamb was not only
slain but came back to life. His death and resurrection therefore go together in their commemoration. St. Paul said, "He
was delivered up for our sins and rose for our justification."
Both elements must be there: death and resurrection. They
belong together. We are saved not by Christ's death alone,
but by both his death and his resurrection.

In the Old Testament Passover feast, a lamb was slain and
by his blood the people were freed from Egypt. In the New
Testament Passover—Easter—a Lamb was slain and then
arose from the dead, and thus by his blood we were freed
from the slavery of sin and ignorance.

The Jews remembered that first Passover by a special feast
every year. Christians now remember that New Testament
Passover by the feast of Easter, but even more importantly,
by every Mass. The Sacrifice of the Mass, since it is a renewal

[5] *Ibid.,* p. 142.

of the sacrifice of "the Lamb of God," is meant to be a superior kind of passover feast, a commemoration of the death and resurrection of Jesus.

> Therefore, O Lord . . . recalling the holy passion and also the resurrection from the dead and the ascension of Christ, we your servants, with your holy people, offer to your resplendent majesty—from your own gifts bestowed upon us—the sacrifice that is perfect. . . .

These words follow the Consecration of every Mass even today. As we use them in our own prayers, we will grow in understanding of the Mass and of what Christ has done for us—both died for us and rose for us. The death and the resurrection go together. The Mass commemorates both.

It may surprise us to learn that for almost a thousand years the normal posture of people at Mass was standing. They understood that standing symbolized resurrection. Since, as St. Paul says, we have all risen with Christ, the custom in the Church was to stand up as if you were a man who had risen from the dead with Christ. We may follow the same custom privately, if we wish.

The celebration of Mass was not an everyday affair in those early days. Only on Sundays and on feast days was the Eucharist celebrated, even though people often received Holy Communion every day. But every Sunday was considered a "Resurrection Day." That was the name given to the day by the early Christians. In the Russian language today this is still the ordinary name for Sunday. Even in the West the custom of calling Sunday "the Day of Resurrection" lasted until the ninth century.

The Roman Rite of the Mass, obviously many years out-of-date even in translation, still stands like a cathedral, venerable in its ancientness and rich in values that are in short supply today. Our searches through the Mass text will give us assurance that, for all the need there is for change, the Latin Mass was magnificently wrought, with a dignity and restraint that explain its durability and the reverence people of so many cultures have given it. The more we come to understand the Latin Mass and its translations, the more we see why it has resisted change, how many men who appreciated its beauties found it almost wholly satisfactory, the disadvantages of small anachronisms being counterweighed, in their judgment, by the essential clarity and grace of the traditional ritual.

And however much we change our ritual (for even great cathedrals grow old and must come down), there will inevitably be anachronisms in it or elements that seem second-best. Perhaps after meditation they will not seem so second-best. At any rate, the liturgy, new or old, belongs to the whole Church, and our first duty in any age will be to accept it and treasure it and try to know it and carry it out as it is. Changes will come. In the meantime, let the liturgy teach us to pray.

> *I will offer the sacrifice of thanksgiving, and I will call upon the name of the Lord* (Ps. 115:8).

19 Submitting to Scripture

My word is a fire, says the Lord, a hammer to break rocks in pieces (Jer. 23:29, Knox).

METHOD: To open the Scriptures and allow them to judge us, not in the hope of putting an evaluation on our own character, but to show us, first, God in Christ, then "Christ in us, our hope of glory." In this large context, we can begin to understand our creaturehood, our sinfulness, and our ideal. It prepares us for confession.

No one can predict the end of the world, not even the angels (Mark 13:32). But one important feature of the day is quite predictable: the element of surprise. In the Last Judgment described by Jesus in St. Matthew's Gospel, both the saved and the lost are surprised, surprised not so much by the fact of their fate as by the standard used in judging them. "Lord, when did we see you hungry and gave you no food?" the lost will ask. And the saved will ask, "Lord, when did we see you hungry, and gave you food?" The unexpected rule of judgment: the way they had treated other men was the way they had treated Christ.

But were they not forewarned of the law according to

which they would be judged? Indeed they were, as the Lord told the lost Dives who begged a chance to come back to earth and warn his brothers of God's surprising law: "They have Moses and the Prophets" (a phrase meaning the Sacred Scriptures). "If they will not believe these, they will not believe a man come back from the dead" (cf. Luke 16:31).

Today we have "Moses and the Prophets" too, as well as the One of whom Moses and the Prophets spoke: the Word of Truth, the Messiah. We have him in many forms—in the Church, in all the sacraments, in the word of preaching. But it is in the Bible that we have our most convenient access to him. And, as is always said but worth repeating, the Bible is not a book we judge, but a book that judges us. We may put it to work judging us then. Perhaps this will somewhat reduce our own surprise on Judgment Day.

In this meditation method we open the Bible and try to see our place in the redemption, to get a sharper and sharper concept of our life work as a part of the whole drama. Our reading may involve such a simple thing as finding ways to improve ourselves, but that is hardly a start. The reading may also be an excellent preparation for confession, especially if examining my conscience has become routine and seldom convinces me of sin. "It may well be, therefore, that the fact that 'I have nothing of importance to reproach myself with' rests on a deep misconception, that it is an indication that my conscience judges by very rough standards, perhaps quite false ones, without being aware of it, as compared with those of God's word."[1] But above all we may use this prayer method to revive our awareness of the living God, of Christ, and of the Christian ideal.

[1] *Prayer*, p. 184. Von Balthasar develops this idea on p. 100 and again on pp. 184 ff., with some examples.

We must avoid mere introspective self-judgment. Anything more than the roughest and most admittedly superficial evaluation of ourselves is futile and a waste of time.[2] We may, however, "examine our conscience," and we should do so regularly and thoroughly and humbly and with the help of the Scriptures. Christ waits for us in the sacrament of penance, ready with his judgment, forgiveness and guidance. But we do not really evaluate ourselves when we examine our consciences, except to admit that our lives are full of weakness and sin and emptiness and hopelessness without his grace. We do not attempt a guess at how we stack up against others or where we have risen to in the spiritual life. And for three reasons: (1) St. Paul warns us against it; (2) true and valid evaluation can only be passed on the whole of life; and (3) the fact that when I try to look at myself, my eyes are clouded by the very faults I am trying to look at. One thing lies open to us, and it is the only thing that matters *now:* in the words of St. Paul:

I press on hoping that I may lay hold of that for which Christ Jesus has laid hold of me [my mission in life]. . . .One thing I do: forgetting what is behind, I strain forward to what is before, I press on towards the goal, to the prize of God's heavenly call in Christ Jesus. (Phil. 3:12–14)

We may choose to approach the Scriptures line by line.

[2] "The person who fixes his gaze on himself in order to know himself better, and so, perhaps, effects a moral improvement, will certainly not encounter God. If he desires to find God's will for him, he must set about this task differently. But whoever seriously seeks God's will in his word will find himself incidentally, and in so far as is necessary." *Prayer,* p. 94.

There is nourishment for man in every word that comes forth from the mouth of God. For example, we open up the first epistle of St. Peter. In chapter 1, at verse 4, we read of "an incorruptible inheritance reserved for you in heaven." We see, with the help of this line, that our hopes until now have been too this-worldly. At verse 5, we read "By the power of God you are guarded through faith for salvation." We receive a new reason for confidence in God. He is guarding us. The Scriptures accuse me of diffidence. At verse 9, we read of "the final issue of your faith, the salvation of your souls." Faith is temporary. Why give it grudgingly?

This kind of line-by-line search for guidance and judgment is also fruitful when applied to the gospels. In the first chapter of St. John, at verse 3, "All things were made through him": I expand my admiration of the Incarnate Word, for the same person is also the world's creator. At verse 12, "To as many as received him, he gave the power of becoming sons of God": I must often receive the Word, in Scripture, in preaching, in the Eucharist. At verse 15, "John bore witness concerning him": and I must likewise bear him witness.

Scattered reading—reading here and there—is also not without its value. "Bear with one another and forgive one another, if anyone has a grievance against any other, even as the Lord has forgiven you, so also do you forgive" (Col. 3:13): here is the world's key to peace. The text accuses me, and yet I blame war and hatred on others only. "It is from the heart's overflow that the mouth speaks. . . . In the day of judgment, men will be brought to account for every thoughtless word they have spoken." (Matt. 12:35–37, Knox) Enough said.

This sort of "searching the Scriptures" can be very profitable and can open the way to contemplation. In this style of scripture reading there are two major mistakes to avoid. First, we must not think that our religion is primarily a moral system concerned with doing good and avoiding evil. It is rather an invitation to faith and total commitment to the person of God, who approaches us in Christ. And we are saved not so much because we become good people (above all, not because we become "nice people") but because, by the free mercy of God inspiring us to "faith which works through charity," we are "formed in the image of his Son."

And the second thing to avoid is such a private reading of the Book that we ignore the Book's owner and interpreter, which is the teaching Church. Every Christian individual possesses the Spirit of Truth, but in different ways, according to their commissions or missions from God. Our bishops and our Holy Father are "clothed with power" to define infallibly what Catholics believe.

Nevertheless, this sort of "searching the Scriptures"—line by line—can be very profitable, given the ordinary precautions, and can open the way to contemplation. Ideally, however, this searching of the Bible should come only after a wider reading or, even better, the study of a commentary on the passage we are to read.

The full sweep of the gospel story is particularly powerful in judging us. Jesus himself judges us, and it is both his divinity and his humanity that convict us of sin. It is foolish, of course, ever to consider his two natures as separate. But there are times in the gospels when the divinity "hides itself" and times when his plain manhood flashes out with a clear brilliance to judge us.

This is especially clear in his clashes with his opponents. For Jesus was a revolutionary in the realm of the spirit against the tyranny and pretense of Israel's priest-politicians.

He openly called them liars, vipers, thieves, sons of the devil. He announced that the judgment of the world had been given to him "by my Father," then he handed that judgment over to the poor and the naked and the hungry—to the masses: "What you do to them, you do to me." "My word is a fire," said God, in the book of Jeremias. "I came to hurl fire on the earth," said Jesus. If we go close to the Word, the fire will test and judge us.

The eventual execution of Jesus was monstrously unjust, but it was hardly unprovoked. He had aligned himself with the masses, and these masses favored him for king. That meant a revolution was threatened. But what provoked the death sentence most of all was his direct attack on the estab- lishment, the Pharisees: on their pride, wealth, cruelty and hypocrisy; and above all his attack on their religious values, claiming that they violated their own law: "You pay tithes on mint and anise and cummin and neglect the weightier things of the Law: justice and mercy and faith." "You lay heavy burdens on men's backs and will not lift a finger to help them." "You devour the substance of widows under pretense of long prayers." "You nullify the commands of God to keep tradition." "You declare yourself just in the sight of men, but God knows your heart." A man who speaks like this to us can only be removed entirely or surrendered to. We either judge him or allow him to judge us.

His divinity judges us too. For the Man in every event is God. In Newman's words:

An individual, Self-dependent, All-perfect, Unchange- able Being; intelligent, living, personal and present; almighty, all-seeing, all-remembering; between whom and His creatures there is an infinite gulf; who has no origin, who is all-sufficient for Himself; who created and upholds the universe. . . . One in whose hands are all things, who has a purpose in every event and a standard for every deed. . . . All that is good, all that is true, all that is beautiful, all that is beneficent, be it great or small, be it perfect or fragmentary, natural as well as supernatural, moral as well as material, comes from Him.[3]

In his resurrection his humanity "hides," and we are offered another word and asked to believe. And again we find ourselves given a choice, to judge the word or reject it; or to believe it and be judged by it, judged small, as God in proportion is large, mighty, infinite; but also judged to be brothers and co-heirs with the risen God-man.[4]

[3] *The Idea of a University* (London, 1898), p. 64.

[4] We may note in passing that our life of prayer itself is often "judged" by the witness of Jesus. The gospel events often show Jesus at prayer, especially in St. Luke. Father Lebreton lists eleven instances: "Every one of Jesus' decisive steps is preceded by a long prayer: He prays at the baptism (Luke 3:21). Then He retires into the desert, led by the Holy Spirit, and spends forty days there. After the first day's sojourn at Capharnaum, before beginning the evangelization of Galilee, He retires long before daybreak into a desert place to pray (Mark 1:35). A little while later, He heals a leper, the crowds come flocking and throng about Him; He retires apart to pray (Luke 5:16). He passes the night in prayer before choosing His apostles (Luke 6:12). After the multiplication of the loaves, in the thick of the Galilean crisis, He retires to pray on the mountain (Mark 6:46). He prays apart before Peter's confession (Luke 9:18). It is in prayer that He is transfigured (Luke 9:29). He prays for Peter at the Last Supper (Luke 22:32). He prays in the Garden (Luke 22:41). He prays on the cross (Luke 23:34–40)." Jules Lebreton, *The Spiritual Teaching of the New Testament* (Westminster: Newman, 1960), p. 216.

And Father Prat provides us with this survey of a similar witness in the life of St. Paul. ". . . The Acts reveal him to us as praying in all

When we come to St. Paul and the epistles, we enter a very wide context. Perhaps you have noticed how St. Paul, for all his writing about Christ, seems to take no notice of the detailed events of Christ's life. He could not be expected to have read the gospel books, of course, for his epistles were written before the gospels. However, he was acquainted with the apostles. He must have heard their preaching. Why does he not preach similarly?

The reason seems to be that it was St. Paul's charismatic gift to have understood with particular clarity the over-all, cosmic plan of God. It was the death and resurrection of Christ that was, above all, significant:

Who shall make accusation against the elect of God? It is God who justifies! Who shall condemn? It is Christ Jesus who died, yes, and rose again, he who is at the right hand of God, who also intercedes for us! Who shall separate us from the love of Christ? (Rom. 8:33–35)

---

the serious circumstances of his life; at the moment when he goes to Ananias to be baptized by him (Acts 9:11), in the Temple after his conversion (22:17), before receiving the laying on of hands (13:3), when he appoints *elders* for the new churches (14.22), in the prison at Philippi (16:25), at Miletus before the assembled elders (20:36), when saying farewell to the Christians of Tyre (21:5), after his miracle at Mitylene (28:8), and at the Three Taverns on the road to Rome (28:15). He prays for his disciples (Rom. 1:9–10, etc.) and for the Jews (Rom. 10:1); he prays also for himself (2 Cor. 12:8; 1 Thess. 3:10); he exhorts the faithful to pray frequently (Rom. 12:12, etc.) and for him (Rom. 15:30, etc.); and relies upon their prayers (Phil. 1:19; Philem. 22). We know that, like the pious Jews of his time, he was accustomed to pray before meals (Acts 27:35)." Fernand Prat, *The Theology of St. Paul,* trans. by John L. Stoddard (Westminster: Newman, 1927), Vol. II, p. 340. (Not all Father Prat's scripture references are given.)

Again, it is not Christ's impoverishment at Bethlehem that affects Paul so much as the fundamental impoverishment in God's Son taking the form of man. "For you know the graciousness of our Lord Jesus Christ—how, being rich, he became poor for your sakes, that by his poverty you might become rich" (2 Cor. 8:9).

The epistles, written before the gospels and being larger in scope, may well be read first. They have something to give us that is not so apparent in the gospels. But in both there is an immense wealth of matter, and great treasures of guidance and judgment to be found.

In your meditation, then, put the Bible before you, recalling that it is a sacred book. Prepare yourself as you usually do before spending time with God, saying short prayers for the success of your meditation. Then open the book and let it do its work of judging. It may help to have a pencil in hand so that you can underline a word, check an important sentence, circle a key phrase or one that connects to some other phrase nearby. You may jot words in the margin or write out insights along the top or bottom of the page. Or with the pencil, you may write out in concrete language your new-found or renewed ideals. Or you may turn the phrases that strike you into decisions or resolutions: Even when we know that the ideal or decision is way out of our reach, it helps sometimes to see what our resolution should be or some day could be.

For an example of what I mean, taking scripture lines used earlier in this chapter, I might write "I must come to consider myself a wealthy man since I have 'an incorruptible inheritance' reserved in heaven." Or another example, "I should have no more extreme fears about the family, because 'by the power of God [we] are guarded through faith for salvation.' "

Whether we use this method in preparing for the sacrament of penance, or for an ordinary longer or shorter period of meditation, what we are doing is not simply making a study of the Bible. "Searching the Bible" is a better expression. We are hunting for ideas and ideals worth living for. We are looking for light, and the light is Christ.

Once we find him, once an idea becomes especially clear or a decision finds its way into our heart, there we pause in our meditation and raise our face to God, and our heart and our mind. There is no need and no advantage in rushing on. We have found God. We face him and we realize that he has also turned his face to us. To break this contact would be, at least, discourteous. It is also foolish, for prayer methods can do no more for us than this, no more than bring us into contact with God. When we have found him—and it may occur immediately—remain there, resting in that striking idea or that moving resolution that brought us into his presence.

There is a natural rhythm to this kind of prayerful pause, and its force may be soon spent and we may be back with the words of the Bible again. But do not hurry. Contemplation should not be aimed at something outside itself, at some product, at a sermon or a book or a conversation. This does not mean that contemplation is irrelevant to daily life, or that we may not be contemplative about our work or our family. What it does mean, and what contemplative people realize almost without being told, is that resolutions or new ideas are not absolutely essential to prayer, that there is a contemplative worship of God which is complete in itself. It does not have to be offered up for any intention, or ever be used in conversation or preaching, or ever be thought of again. And we must leave an opening for this, for it is God at his closest and most real.

My word is a fire, says the Lord, a hammer to break rocks in pieces (Jer. 23:29, Knox).

20 Speaking without Speech

The Lord is near. Have no anxiety, . . . and may the peace of God which surpasses all understanding guard your hearts and minds in Christ Jesus. (Phil. 4:6–7)

METHOD: To simply put yourself in the presence of God without saying much or going through much of a reasoning process or looking for any resolutions to make. Give God your quiet faith and your uncomplicated openness and realize how he looks at you with a father's care, a brother's understanding, a friend's encouragement and love. This is called the prayer of simplicity.

The most simple things in life are often the hardest to define or describe: a breath, a sound, a scent. When prayer becomes simple, its explanations become complicated. But we take up the task, for it is one of the most important in this book.

I believe there are many forms of this "prayer of simplicity." The essence of all the forms is the state of mental and volitional simplicity and quiet. If you are the kind of person who can sit for a while and enjoy the sight of a lovely landscape, you have some idea of the prayer of simplicity. Or, if you can find contentment in walking along a beach in the evening, enjoying the harmony between your own body and soul and the sounds and colors and sensations of the seaside, you can understand what the prayer of simplicity is. If you can enjoy the sound of musical harmony or, on occasion, the near-perfect consonance of music with its audience, with its subject, with the times; or if you know what is meant by grief too deep for words, or beauty beyond description, or a poem that takes your breath away, or a thrilling idea, you can understand this form of prayer. If you are content at times to sit wordlessly by and enjoy the mere presence of a person you love, while others are talking to him—after a long separation, perhaps—then, if you believe in God, you can also pray the prayer of simplicity.

This simple contact with God that we are speaking of is like these ordinary experiences, but different from them also. These examples give us some idea of the simplicity and insight and wordlessness of the prayer of simplicity. But there is something more to it.

Here is the central point. There are times in all of our lives when the scattered things we have learned about God come together in our mind. God ceases to be merely a subject we study, and he becomes "Thou, my God," and that is enough. Suddenly there is a kind of clearness and simplicity about things that have been foggy until now or contradictory or not related to each other at all. I come to realize that this One that I am thinking about is present, is within me and all around me, has turned his face toward me and is regarding me, has a care for me and blesses me. And for a moment or for a few minutes, or even a longer time, I attend to his regard and his presence without words, or at least without any attempt at adequate words. Perhaps

I repeat a simple prayerful phrase again and again as Christ did in praying so simply in Gethsemani. This may be called the prayer of simplicity.

This prayer takes different forms and is given a number of names: the prayer of faith, the prayer of simple regard, the prayer of quiet. It is a part of almost all contemplative prayer. Some Christians pray this way from their earliest days or from the day of their conversion. The New Testament gives us many examples of it. For instance, Peter's words, "Lord, it is good for us to be here," just after Jesus' transfiguration. The words were near nonsense, and a smile or shout would have expressed the same sentiment. It was a prayer of simplicity. And the way Peter must have prayed as he watched the crucifixion from afar off may well have been "the prayer of faith."

When Magdalene saw the risen Jesus and said, "Rabbi!"— this was simple face-to-face prayer, "the prayer of simple regard." We may find "the prayer of quiet" in Mary of Bethany as she sat at the Master's feet, day after day. And the wordless exchange between the child Jesus and his mother as she was straightening out his clothes for him after a day playing with the other village children—this was the same sort of prayer. They look at each other and words are unnecessary or irrelevant or impossible.

For Father Teilhard de Chardin, whose ideas and words have appeared so often in this book, the prayer of simplicity must have come quite easily. He was able to see God in everything in the world. Matter, which for us is often so opaque, and suffering and growth and work, which for us are often so incomprehensible, were "diaphanous" for him. They were nothing but a veil of such delicate and fine a texture as to be transparent: "If we may slightly alter a hallowed expression, we could say that the great mystery of Christianity is not exactly the appearance [the Epiphany of our Lord] but the transparence of God in the Universe—his diaphany."[1] For Teilhard, God was all around him, and Christ was the center drawing everything together. Teilhard lived, and has taught us that we live, in a milieu of God, a divine milieu.

When it comes to the problem of how you and I can learn to practice this form of prayer, it may help us to approach the method from another aspect. Consider the question of why people object to "candid cameras." The answer is, I suppose, that there is really something quite unfair about observing a person without his knowledge. But why? Because most of us act differently when we are being watched. This is often obvious with children, but it is even more true of adults. If we know we are alone and are unobserved, we all have a comfortable and relaxed way of acting. But when we, say, pick up the phone and experience even this limited contact with another, the situation changes radically and so do we. To hear someone else speaking to

---

[1] Quoted from *The Divine Milieu*, p. 130, by Robert T. Francoeur, "The Cosmic Piety of Teilhard de Chardin," *Catholic Mind*, December 1964, p. 6. An editor's note appended to the text of *The Divine Milieu* (p. 46) quotes the following expansion of the diaphany concept, taken from an autobiographical work: "*Throughout my* life, *by means of* my life, the world has little by little caught fire in my sight until, aflame all around me, it has become almost completely luminous from within. . . . Such has been my experience in contact with the earth— the diaphany of the Divine at the heart of the universe on fire . . . Christ; his heart; a fire; capable of penetrating everywhere and, gradually, spreading everywhere." The Jesuit poet Gerard Manley Hopkins came close to the same idea when he wrote, in his *Notebooks*, "All things therefore are charged with love, are charged with God, and if we know how to touch them, give off sparks and take fire, yield drops and flow, ring and tell of Him." *The Notebooks and Papers of Gerard Manley Hopkins,* ed. by Humphrey House (New York: Oxford, 1937), p. 68. (Cited by Martz, *The Poetry of Meditation,* p. 322).

us personally, and to be heard by them in return, pulls us together sharply, wakes us up, sets our psyche in motion. It seems to change everything. Then to go a further step, when there is another person actually looking at us, regarding us intently, or when there are two or three or a number of persons doing the same: we know we have come into another, still more radically different, set of circumstances. If an observer is unfriendly, we withdraw if we can. But when the person looking at us is open and friendly and accepting, and when that person is very important to us, someone we admire and love, then a unique psychological phenomenon takes place. We are suddenly at our best. A kind of alertness and self-possession and simplicity comes over us. We are at once quiet and intense, unselfconscious, open and uninhibited.

This sets the stage for the prayer of simplicity. With eyes of faith I look at God and know God looks at me. We are present to one another. We meet, face each other. Without words and in a flash—though there is nothing miraculous about it—my heart is understood by his and his by me. God becomes "My God, Thou."

No spiritual writer, to my knowledge, has explained this so well as von Hildebrand in his book *Transformation in Christ.* He says:

In our contemplative surrender to the absolute Person, we experience the light of His loving glance penetrating our soul, and are conscious of His personal response to our loving surrender. . . . We may dwell in God with that absolute, changeless tranquillity which is alien to the precious, condensed "supreme moments" in the spiritual relationship between finite personal beings joined in mutual awareness of one another. God the omnipresent, who pervades all presentness, is also the eternal Being, towering above time in its entirety; He unites the concentrated actuality of the "supreme moment" to the timelessness of unaltered super-actuality. . . .[2]

And so, for instance, we may find we can pray very simply when we reflect on the most basic things we know about the Divine Being: God is Power, God is Love, God is Wisdom. Our Father has all power, everything is in his control. The Holy Spirit is love, and love asks for no excuses, will not even allow them. The Son of God, our co-heir and brother, God's Word, is infinite Wisdom and Understanding, and he opens our mind and heart as easily as he opens the palm of his hand. So, from outside us, nothing to fear. From inside us, no shame, no hesitation. We are face to face with God, without any need or even inclination to speak, for everything is already understood. We simply rest in his presence or walk in his presence as Adam did, or work in his presence.

It seems at times like no prayer at all, but it is a very fine prayer. It must not be confused with daydreaming, or its simplicity equated with boredom or mental blankness or sleepiness. Its great distinguishing mark is alertness. Anything that tends to put us to sleep or in which we lose interest or experience boredom is not the prayer of simplicity. A sleep-inducing activity cannot be man functioning at his best, cannot be contemplation.

Contemplation then is never idle; it has no wish to "doze" in the presence of the beloved, it is ever on the alert to feed on "every word that proceeds from the

[2] Dietrich von Hildebrand, *Transformation in Christ* (New York: Taplinger, Image Edition, 1963), p. 120.

mouth of God." Yet it is never curious or insatiable, but knows how to prize and be content with the word and the food of the moment. . . . As time goes on, it learns to do with less and less matter in contemplation —it comes to see and grasp in each detail all its depth of meaning. The "prayer of quiet" once attained with the help of grace, extension is replaced by intensity; the roving discourse of the mind is replaced by a kind of intuition. . . .[3]

We cannot always pray this way, and some of us can pray this way only very seldom indeed, and only for a short time. Others find it the easiest of all methods. It is mostly a matter of temperament and grace. The Holy Spirit cannot be limited in his action, but usually he makes use of our ordinary human talents, and we pray, and should pray, pretty much the way we do other things.

We should be content with the way we can pray at the moment, and not try methods of prayer just because they may be called "higher forms." This would be a mistake and a sin of pride. We are ready to admit that animals can thrive only in their natural habitat. Some were born for the trees, some for rocky places, some for a warm and productive life underground. And so it is with the souls of men. Some thrive in a free and windy climate, some on the ledges and cliffs of life, some in the methodical step-by-step way of life mostly hidden. Our prayer should be of the same fabric as our lives.

But God "visits" all of us at times. Sometimes at our prayer, sometimes, just for a moment, right in the middle of work or while we are boarding a bus or singing cowboy songs with a group of friends.

[3] *Prayer,* p. 106.

A good friend of mine told me once about what he considered to have been a visit of God. He was at a party, he began—and as he told this to me he turned his head and looked off into space as if seeing it all again. He could recall all the details: who was there, and with whom, the noise, the music, the atmosphere of gaiety and friendship, the laughing and loud conversation. Suddenly it was time for dinner, and as people began to move in toward the dining room, a sudden and unmistakable feeling or experience of emptiness came over him: a sense of darkness, void, nothingness. The party was at its height and it meant nothing to him. Then, out of the void, rose a quiet yearning for God, and then calmly and suddenly God was there, present to him, the living God, the Father, the all-powerful, all-satisfying God. And he went in to dinner, he said, a changed man.

In that brief moment, my friend had encountered God, met him in faith face-to-face. It was a moment of simplicity and intensity and quiet. He had received a kind of bread the others "knew not of"—a holy communion with God— and it took away all the hunger and emptiness he had felt.

This is the way the prayer of simplicity is. It is hard to plan. Life's best moments are most often unexpected, or happen spontaneously from the chance chemistry of several otherwise normal elements. So with this prayer. We are ready for it in every meditation, ready to meet God however he may come, waiting for him. Meanwhile, we search.

> *The Lord is near. Have no anxiety, . . . and may the peace of God which surpasses all understanding guard your hearts and minds in Christ Jesus.* (Phil. 4:6–7)